The Dice of Life
And The Roll They Play

Howard Minor

Copyright © 2023 Howard Minor

All rights reserved.

Explanation of survivorship bias excerpt credited to Dean Yeong.

Cover Design By: Piere d'Arterie

Paperback ISBN: 979-8-9876250-0-2
Ebook ISBN: 979-8-9876250-1-9

First Edition April 2023

www.howardminor.com
Contact: HowardMinor@HowardMinor.com

CONTENTS

How the Dice Work 1

Build Your Character 13

The Game Board 27

Upgrades 41

Number Bias 51

Life Isn't Fair 65

Getting Motivated 73

Survivorship Bias 87

The Dark Dice 95

Putting It All Together 101

ACKNOWLEDGMENTS AND DEDICATION

As we travel through this unbelievable adventure in life, there are angels who appear on our journey to help carry us along the way. Certain people who force the question of how you would survive without them. At least for me and my family, my wife Jennifer has been that foundational pillar on which everything else has stood. For us to survive through our most difficult times, we were forced to create our own inside "language" to help clearly define and explain the pain and challenges that continually formed around us. Using the concept of a pair of dice gave us a tool to better understand the world and why people behave the way they do.

We hope this perspective can offer the same insights and assurances that helped us along our way.

I dedicate this book and my life to her.

.

1

How the Dice Work

Games and Dice

Games! There are all kinds of them. Card games, board games, puzzles, adventure, computer games, or even imaginary guessing games. Even if you haven't played a game recently, most of us have a handful of fond memories about a fun game we used to play when we were younger. Maybe with your family, friends, neighbors, or even by yourself.

Growing up in a household of 4 boys, my brothers and I would go through these stages occasionally, where we would get hooked on a certain board game and repeatedly play it every chance we could. We would find some random game in the closet that one of us had gotten for Christmas and then every day we would play that same game for hours and hours until we either got sick of it or each other. The real problem was that we were all VERY competitive. So, these happy innocent fun little games quickly became sessions of a brutal focused attack on each other. It got ugly!! We were relentless with strategies, smack talking, gambling, and often high stakes for the winners and losers. I still have memories of doing many extra chores because of landing on those stupid hotels.

The truth is that games play a critical role in our social and personal development as human beings. Of course, they're fun for a few minutes. But we actually NEED that exposure to competition in our lives to provide us with challenges and obstacles that we will face in the real world. Games serve as a safe zone for us to focus our minds and bodies in some sort of struggle to overcome challenges that will inevitably come our way. We learn how to be resilient when we're behind. We learn how to make decisions that will affect us later in the game. We learn how to play offense and when to play defense. We learn how to implement and execute different strategies. We learn how to win and hopefully how to lose. We also learn about taking chances and letting fate decide the outcome for many of our decisions.

But the one thing that most of the great classical games have in common is the essential element of chance. In most games, this usually takes the form of something like drawing a card from a pile or waiting to see what the dice will give you when you roll. So, it's by no accident that most board games are driven by nothing more than a simple pair of dice. A standard 6-sided cube specifically designed to give you a random number between 1 and 6. A pair of them will give you a number between 2 and 12. Dice introduce the foundation of unexpected chaos. An unpredictable outcome with every roll making each game a unique experience every time. This, of course, makes the game much more fun because you never know what to expect. You never know what those pesky dice may give you when it's your turn. It may grant you with something good! While at the same time possibly revealing a number you may dread!

Probabilities

We're going to refer to this dice analogy throughout this book so it's a good idea if we take some time to review our high school statistics class on the subject.

We'll start by reviewing the basic probabilities when rolling a standard pair of 6-sided dice:

Dice Total	Odds	Percent
2	1 in 36	2.8%
3	1 in 18	5.6%
4	1 in 12	8.3%
5	1 in 9	11.1%
6	1 in 7.2	13.9%
7	1 in 6	16.7%
8	1 in 7.2	13.9%
9	1 in 9	11.1%
10	1 in 12	8.3%
11	1 in 18	5.6%
12	1 in 36	2.8%

Looking at this table immediately pushes us into the domain of understanding the concept of probabilities. Because of basic mathematics and the unchangeable laws of the universe, some totals are just more likely to occur than others. It doesn't matter what you WANT to happen, or what you think is fair. It's the natural law of physics and the ultimate result of random probability. So, understanding the likelihood of these outcomes becomes important when playing certain types of board games. It can greatly affect your strategy when you understand that some of these numbers will eventually turn up more than others.

Monopoly

Most people are at least somewhat familiar with the classic board game of Monopoly. It has become the grandfather example of learning about real estate asset ownership and basic banking operations. Everyone typically wants to own Boardwalk and Park Place since those are the high ticket, high reward spaces on the board. Most players immediately look at those high rent numbers and they get excited because they can't wait for someone to give them a huge payday!! (Or in my case do extra chores for them.) But it's well documented that the real secret of this game exists with the seemingly mediocre orange spaces. (New York, Tennessee, and St. James if you are familiar). There are a few economic reasons for this. But the biggest reason is simply because of where they exist beyond the jail space. Because of the "Go To Jail" space, rolling too many doubles, and the chance card rules, most players end up in jail at least two or three times during the course of a normal game. So, you can use that fact to your advantage by owning the properties that have the greatest chance of someone landing on them once they get out of jail. Look at the table above and you'll see why.

From the Jail square:
- St. James = 6 spaces (13.9%)
- Tennessee = 8 spaces (13.9%)
- New York = 9 spaces (11.1%)

That's a 38.9% chance that someone will land on an orange square coming out of jail! Of course, it's never a guarantee, but it's a classic example of how you can use probability to your advantage and build your strategy using basic statistics.

Yahtzee

Another example that really starts to leverage the beautiful randomness of a set of dice is the classic game of Yahtzee. This was and still is a favorite among my gambling addicted brothers. Between them, no less than several thousands of dollars have changed hands because of this infamous game.

If you're unfamiliar, this game is played by taking turns rolling 5 dice which is the only equipment needed. The basic premise is to collect a certain number of combinations each time you roll the dice. (3 of a kind, a straight, full house, etc...) These combinations have different point values based on how rare or difficult they are to happen. So, the entire strategy is based on understanding and making decisions about the probability of these various combinations. Obviously, the prize of this game is rolling all dice of the same number which is called a Yahtzee. (Very low probability, but of course worth the most points.)

But the interesting thing about Yahtzee is that your statistical decisions may also depend on what your opponent is doing. For example, if they got lucky with one of their combinations early in the match, that may put them ahead and force you to take more risk than you normally would otherwise. To be truly successful in this game, it is very necessary to adjust the risks you take based on factors outside your own dice!

But the underlying factor is that you still never know for sure what's going to happen. There is always an element of unpredictability that enhances the fun of any game like this one. You can strategize, prepare, and calculate all you want, but you will always be at the mercy of what the dice will give you. We'll come back to this point later.

Role Playing Adventure Games

Beyond Yahtzee and the standard board games that involve a simple pair of dice for movement on a path, there are several games that take the random unpredictability of dice rolling to its fullest potential. These are games that are generally much more complex in their rules and objectives. It's important to take some time to understand how these types of games work, because they provide a beautiful analogy to understanding how random chance and probabilities can affect our lives in the real world.

For example, Dungeons and Dragons is one of the most famous role-playing adventure games of all time. You may have played this as a kid, or at least made fun of the kids that did. This is a popular old fantasy game that exists in an imaginary world involving a complex story full of challenges, adventures, and situations that are only limited by someone's imagination. Instead of a standard playing board where you march around on a path of predetermined spaces, you immerse yourself into entire fantasy worlds full of monsters, weapons, spells, different languages, creatures, and magic. During the game, you will be faced with a series of imaginary situations and challenges based on an overarching story. You are then forced to make different decisions about which path to take or which quest to follow. The lure of the game is that you explore this fantasy world by interacting with various objects and characters with always unpredictable results.

To play these types of games, the first step is usually to create an imaginary character that you will control throughout the adventure. You will continually make decisions about what this character will do and how it will interact with objects and other players as you explore this fantasy world.

An essential part of this typical character-building process is to initially determine the starting point of 6 key attributes.

- Strength - A measure of muscle and physical stamina: Helps your character with the ability to carry items and engage in physical combat.

- Dexterity - Additional physical attributes such as hand-eye coordination, agility, and reflexes: Helps with certain types of combat that require quicker or more agile movements.

- Constitution - Describes a character's toughness and resistance to things like disease and poison which can occur during your journey: Constitution can be helpful in raising the number of hit points you can withstand and how long you can last during combat or a tough situation.

The Dice of Life

- Intelligence - Ability to reason and how quickly you can learn something new: Will help you learn new skills quickly and cheaply.

- Wisdom - Willpower and intuition: Increases the number of magic spells you can use.

- Charisma - Physical attractiveness and persuasiveness: Can help the effectiveness of certain spells and being persuasive. (Just like in real life, I've seen examples in games where charisma can save you money by getting a better deal at the market!)

D&D fans will quickly point out there's actually a bit more to it than this. But the basic premise to understand here is that you roll a die to determine what your starting "score" is for each of these abilities. This essentially creates the starting point of the abilities with which your character will be playing the game. Because of the random nature of the dice, you will always start the game with a slightly different character every time you play. Because of the random elements of probability, it's very likely you may be strong in one category, but weak in another. These variations of a character create a totally different adventure with unique strategies and outcomes every time.

So why would having different skills and abilities matter in a game like this?

The Dice of Life

How The Role-Playing Dice Work

Well, during the imaginary adventure, you will encounter a variety of situations that will require different skills that may increase your chances of success. For example, you could be faced with a choice of battling a wizard or a snake. You may have a need to learn a new language that will allow you to read a secret scroll to unlock a treasure box or a key. A ghost may be chasing you and you need to cast a spell to protect yourself from that kind of foe. There is no limit to what situations you may encounter or what skills you may require to be successful on this fantasy adventure.

So, these imaginary "battles" or "challenges" are usually performed by rolling a chosen set of dice to determine the outcome. To change the probability even more, the exotic dice in these games can go beyond the standard 6 sides. Often dice with 10 or 20 sides are used to increase the possible ranges of what values could be rolled. Again, the presence of the dice creates an element of chance but can also introduce elements of advantage. The native abilities of your characters may give you a bonus statistical advantage when that distinct skill may prove to be useful in a particular situation. This advantage may come in the form of rolling a larger die, using a number multiplier of some value, or bonus hit points to increase your health or strength. The way this typically works is if your character has a particularly strong ability, you may be allowed to add 3 or 4 points to your roll on a 20-sided die roll while your opponent can not. So, of course, you have a much better chance of rolling a higher number and winning that conflict! Conversely, you may have a situation where your opponent has the bonus advantage. It's still possible you may win in a scenario like that, but you can see how the odds may not necessarily be in your favor. Therefore, that may be a situation you should avoid and will likely change the decision on which path you take on this adventure.

It quickly becomes clear that the native abilities of your imaginary character will have a direct impact on the decisions you make throughout the game. Choosing which path to take or what monster to battle essentially creates the fun of the game. It's generally a good idea to take advantage of what you're good at, while avoiding confrontations where you may have little chance of success. All those decisions and successes are determined by understanding the core probabilities of those dice.

The other great twist about games like this is that you're not always stuck with what you start with. Every time you win a battle or open a box, you may collect experience points or some sort of treasure along the way. When you collect enough rewards, they can be used to 'upgrade' your core abilities. So, the more battles you win and treasures you collect, the better off you are in increasing your abilities to accomplish other tasks in the game. Maybe increase your Wisdom so your spells will have a better chance against that ghost? Maybe increase your dexterity bonus so you'll have more success fighting a quick moving snake who is guarding the key that you need?

What The Dice Mean To Us

Visualizing this type of gameplay and understanding how it works is a fantastic analogy for how randomness and probabilities of dice rolling can work in our own real world lives.

The essence of this dice-rolling game analogy falls into three basic principles which becomes the crux of what this book is about:

1.   We are all born with a random unique set of talents, abilities, aptitudes, and characteristics. Many of these we may be able to improve along the way. But for some, we will always be at the mercy of what we have originally been given.

2.   As we grow through life, we are continually being shaped and molded by another set of circumstances. These include our environment, social influences, education, people close to us, and events that occur to us during our life. They have an enormous impact on creating our values and motivations. Some of these we can control, others we cannot.

3.   No matter our efforts, the results of our journey will always be at the mercy of an unknown outcome. Our goal can never be to guarantee the results. But only to maximize (or minimize) the probability of what occurs.

2

Build Your Character

Let's take the next step by applying these same role-playing concepts to the creation of an actual person in the real world we live in. However, instead of an imaginary character in a fantasy game, we will essentially use that same character-building process to create a new human individual. So just like in the example of our fantasy game, we will begin by selecting a few core 'Abilities' and toss a standard 6-sided die to see what we start out with. The criteria selected below are just a small example of this, and by no means an extensive list.

Rolling a 6 is an outcome of being very good. While rolling a 1 is well, not so good.

The Dice of Life

1. Where were you born?

   - In an affluent neighborhood in a rich country that celebrates individual freedoms with minimal crime and poverty. (6)
   - In the slums of a 3rd world country tormented by a corrupt dictator, gangs, famine, and war. (1)

2. Who were your parents?
   - Well educated, loving, caring, and the innate desire to raise you with healthy habits, ethics, and values. (6)
   - Abusive parents? No parents? No person to guide and care for you and nurture you in your critical developmental years? (1)

3. Genetic Health?
   - Healthy genes, no family history of addiction, disease, or illnesses. (6)
   - Extensive family history of mental health issues, cancer, or hereditary genetic disorders. (1)

4. Intelligence/Wisdom?
   - Naturally smart, learning new skills always comes easy, gifted with insights into how the world works, instinctive ability for mature decision making. (6)
   - Multiple learning disorders, trouble learning how to read, cognitive challenges that prevent even the most basic learning and social functions. (1)

5. Charisma/Looks?
   - You're beautiful! You value good hygiene, a healthy diet, and you're gorgeous without even trying! (6)

- Physical deformities, not physically attractive, people tend to look away when they see you. (1)

Percentage of Dice Totals Distributed Against 5 Attributes

Dice Total	Percentage
5	0.013
6	0.064
7	0.193
8	0.450
9	0.900
10	1.620
11	2.636
12	3.922
13	5.401
14	6.944
15	8.372
16	9.452
17	10.03

Dice Total	Percentage
18	10.03
19	9.452
20	8.372
21	6.944
22	5.401
23	3.922
24	2.636
25	1.620
26	0.900
27	0.450
28	0.193
29	0.064
30	0.013

The Dice of Life

On a graph, the distribution looks like this:

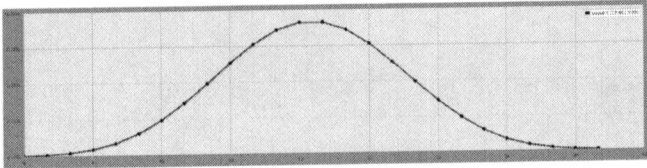

For every 100 people, about 80% will fall with a score between 12 and 22.

The Distribution Of Results

What this graph is demonstrating is that most people will have a combination of these core characteristics occurring somewhere in the middle. Most likely we may be strong in one area, but weak in another. They balance out to somewhat of an average of an overall score.

But what this also tells us is that there will be a few lucky people who will essentially get a Yahtzee with all 6s!! It's not a likely scenario. Only about 2 out of 100. But it WILL statistically happen given enough chances. There are MANY people in this world so given enough time and chances, someone will essentially hit the lottery with their initial starting point. Another interesting fact to consider is that our natural instinct is to immediately start thinking about who we personally know that seems to have rolled all 6s. We get jealous of these people since they got all the breaks! It's not fair! But rarely do we take the time to think about the people that fate assigned to the bottom of this graph. Because of the evenness of the distribution, there are just as many people struggling at the very bottom of these random rolls. Did you catch yourself looking up or down?

The kicker is that with many of these dice rolls, we don't get a second chance to roll them. In many cases, we are stuck with whatever we're given. They essentially become the dice values that we can't ever change. That's an important point to remember.

More Attributes And Skills

Again, by no means are these first 5 attributes an extensive list. They are just a starting example to illustrate the overall point. In fact, it's a necessary next step on this journey to start building a list of additional characteristics and aptitudes that would directly affect the lifestyle and development of our unique human character. Many attributes aren't necessarily good or bad, but they typically have a range of measurement.

Imagine the possibility of variations when adding some of these characteristics and aptitudes into our calculations:

- Athleticism
- Musical Inclination
- Artistic Inclination
- Patience
- Emotional Intelligence
- Risk Tolerance
- Spiritual Sensitivity
- Social Preferences (Introvert vs Extrovert)
- Economics and Resource Management
- Empathy
- Organizational Skills
- Imagination/Creativity
- Leadership
- Mental Health

- Work Ethic
- Mathematics
- Memorization
- Spatial Reasoning
- Competitiveness
- Self Esteem

You'll probably start to imagine where your personal character fits on the scale with some of these. You may have even taken some formalized tests or exams to more accurately measure how you score. But the overall results are usually the same. You may score high on some, but lower on others.

One of the biggest debates in this field is trying to determine which attributes and abilities we are born with and which ones we develop along the way. It's a hot topic that is most difficult to test and know for sure. But comprehensive studies are being conducted all the time with often very surprising results. Is everyone born with the same potential in all categories? What about aptitudes in music or art? What about a strong work ethic or leadership skills? Which items on a list like this are given to us by nature vs. nurture? It's true that we can all work to improve ourselves in any of these areas. But it seems very apparent that some people have a natural distinct advantage when improving in some of these areas over others.

Furthermore, many of these skills are developed and enhanced by our core values. Our core values determine what we believe is important and where we decide to invest our limited time and energy. For example, some people value music over sports. Some people value their career over relationships. So, then we need to ask the next obvious question: Where do our values come from? Are they instilled in us at birth as well; do we choose them along the way; did someone else choose them for us; or most likely, could it be a combination of everything?

And then what about personality types? There are plenty of tools and different surveys that can be very helpful in determining what type of underlying personalities we may fall into. People generally fit into a few broad categories or stereotypes that are familiar to many of us. This information is great because it can give us insight into who we are as individuals and why we act the way we do. Again, we may be able to tweak them a bit, but usually they all stem from some sort of disposition to which we were inherently born with. Or at the very least which values were instilled on us at a young age.

It's also funny how when we take some of those tests with friends or colleagues, they often make so much sense! They clearly show how people are different and explain so much about why people act the way they do. And yet 20 minutes later, we seem to forget about it and go back to treating them the same way we did all along.

Situational Dice

The next set of example attributes that we need to consider for your character fall into somewhat of the situational category. These are the events and circumstances that may or may not happen to you in your life either as a child, teenager, adult, or even today. These examples may not necessarily be measured by a scale. But in most cases, you can't choose how or when they happen to you. Therefore, we find these situations also occurring as yet another random dice roll that we have to deal with.

The Dice of Life

It's very clear that they absolutely affect the development of how you see the world and who you will grow to be.

- Did you have someone in your life encouraging you at a young age? Were you abused, neglected, or ignored?
- Did you get picked on in school? Did you even go to school?
- Were you raised in poverty? Or in wealth?
- Did you grow up in a war zone? Were you close to people that may have been violently injured or killed around you?
- Where you raised in the city? Or on a farm?
- Did something happen to you that affected your ability to have a close relationship with another person?
- Did you witness a tragedy or experience a horrible event that may have traumatized you in some way?
- Were you surrounded by laughter or tears?
- Were you affected in some way by an injury or accident?
- Were you raised to be religious? If so, what religion? Which church?
- What values did your parents instill on you? Did they drive you to be a musician when you didn't want to? Did they drive you to do anything at all?

Children can't choose who their parents are, where they grew up, what their environment was, or typically what happens to them along the way. We often don't get to choose what values are initially instilled in us. Much of life happens to us as a never-ending stream of random chances and experiences. An expanding array of both internal and external probabilities constantly feeding off each other to build us to what we are today. Because of so many variables, we all end up responding to these events in our own unique way. It may help explain why some children accept what their parents taught them while others blatantly reject it.

So Many Dice

The key point to make here is that much of who we are is determined by a huge number of dice rolls. Our human character is the collected results of all these dice building upon themselves and interacting with each other in ways we can't always see or define.

We all know from an early age that people are different, but I think we often make the mistake of not realizing what this truly means and how deep it goes. It's very easy for us to see and observe the external environment of the world around us. We are quick to make judgments or have expectations about how someone should act or feel in a certain situation. But what about all the internal, hormonal, chemical, and natural abilities that are happening within that person that we're not able to see or calculate?

We've only named a few, but it's easy to recognize that there are thousands of these variables of all shapes and sizes molding us to create what we experience as our own unique perspective on life. So, life is not a simple situation of 20 or 30 dice rolls of chance, but of thousands upon thousands. Each with different levels of strength and impact. Again, some you can learn to control and influence, while many you cannot.

Because of all these differences, the results of everything you do and experience will also most certainly be unique. For example, if someone has developed a very sensitive personality, they would be affected by a traumatic situation much differently than someone who has a more refined ability to adapt to an experience like that. Even though two people could experience the exact same situation, that same event may barely slow one person down, but may cause someone else to stop altogether.

Because of their unique point of view, people may not always be able to understand why someone else doesn't respond to a given situation in the exact same way that they do. It happens all the time when we try to expect certain feelings or actions from someone else. Examples: "You SHOULD have felt this way about something!" Or: "You SHOULD have reacted this way when that happened!"

An example of a common argument in many relationships:
- Why don't you care enough about this?
- Why do you care too much about it?

Sometimes it becomes easier to forgive and relate to someone when you understand the source of their behaviors and feelings. We're still responsible for our own actions and words, but it helps our perspective to reflect on the underlying reasons why someone has become the person they are. Most people are not always aware of why they act or feel the way they do, and neither are we.

From Where Do Our Dice Rolls Originate?

Most parents who have multiple kids learn these lessons very quickly. Same environment, same food, same household, yet they can't believe how different their kids are. They each have various personalities and temperaments that they seem to have been born with. If you pay attention to this, you quickly realize that you may need to discipline them differently. They respond to different levels of attention at different times in their lives.

Rewards and chore charts may work great with one child, but not with another. Some kids may need extra help learning how to read or may have the natural need for an entirely different level of emotional support. It's so much more complicated than we assume. Everyone is a good parent ... until they are one!

And so, this brings us back full circle back to the dice rolling of parenting. It's also reasonable to assume that the different temperaments of children will invoke different responses from the same parents. How often do parents recognize and accommodate the different learning styles and emotional needs of their children? Do they encourage them at the right time in just the right way to help maximize their potential and social development in certain areas? Do they say the right motivational words at the right time when their child is in a vulnerable situation? Do they force them in a certain direction because of what THEY think is best? What values are they prioritizing for their children? Do they teach them HOW to think or WHAT to think? Are they too soft when they need to teach more toughness? Are they too aggressive when they need to back off? Do they even care about such things? Are they even aware of them?

It seems to me that we absolutely don't want this reality to be true. It's so inconvenient! It is MUCH easier for us to imagine humans as a simple explainable, predictable machine: a clearly defined object with gears, levers, and switches that all work the same way if we set them all in the same position. Just follow the recipe and get the desired results. We often get locked into the belief that since this solution worked for me, it must also then work for you.

But biology simply doesn't work that way. We often forget that humans are imperfect biological creatures that are given random subtle changes with every birth. These variations between individuals are exactly what allows us to survive and thrive as a species. Some of us are explorers, leaders, thinkers, caregivers, or artists. Our individual unique brain chemistry may be constantly pulling us in a certain direction. That's why we typically do so much better when we are placed in a career or activity that we're naturally good at and enjoy. That's the chemistry in our bodies telling us what we were meant to do, and if that instinctive calling is suppressed or defined by someone else, we can end up miserable, depressed, or worse.

Know The Character You Have To Play The Game With

Like most of us, I was on a mission in my life to be "successful". And from what I was told by the voices and influences in the world around me, that certainly meant being financially wealthy and of course becoming the CEO of some huge company. Because those are the only truly successful people, right?? RIGHT??? That's also probably why the first question someone asks you when they meet is what you do for a living. Unfortunately in our society, it seems to be a quick way to judge how worthy you are.

Early in my career, I made the obvious decision to become an entrepreneur and start my own consulting company. I had become a slick software engineer and very skilled database architect, and I was more than ready to take on this next step. I began the training: hours of research into everything I could learn about how businesses work, marketing techniques, corporate structures, and the key strategies for new startups. I attended business seminars, classes, and anything I could get my hands on to give me an advantage. I did all this because of course I wanted to level up my skills and maximize my chances for success.

But something started to happen as I got deeper into this rabbit hole. I began to get extremely overwhelmed and stressed out. I started to get physically sick, and it took me a while to figure out exactly why. It wasn't entirely because of the workload; (which was unbelievable by the way…), but I began to realize there was a very key skill attribute that is necessary for a journey like that. For me, that missing piece was something called Risk Tolerance. I had stumbled across the discovery that mine was very low. I'm not sure if I was either raised that way or had a natural tendency, or most likely both. It didn't really matter. I was going down a path that my body was simply not designed for. I didn't have the right metabolism, stress tolerance, or mental chemistry to handle the swings and uncertainty that is required of an entrepreneur. The mere thought of taking on enormous bank loans or being responsible for other people's capital investments was simply not something my body was geared to do, especially with a young family at home to take care of. As it turns out, some people love and thrive on it! For them, the same situation amounts to a thrill they can't get enough of. Not that I couldn't change without some really hard work, but I recognized that going down that road was going to be much more difficult for me than possibly others in that same position. It turns out this is a very common outcome for entrepreneurs, one that happens all the time. That's exactly why it becomes so important to know yourself and understand the strengths and weaknesses of your character before you take on a challenge.

Goals are always tough to fight for, but they become tougher when you also must fight yourself along the way.

Unfortunately, nobody talked about this in the business seminars I attended. Those motivational speakers were all psyching us up to go after our financial dreams no matter what. Work hard, don't give up, and you will be rich! That attitude is absolutely necessary!

The reality is that there are several more factors involved here than just a decision and hard work. All those dice rolls start adding up to create the unique circumstances of who we are as a person and exactly what we're trying to accomplish. It's important to always consider the abilities and skills of the character that we're playing this game with. It may directly affect your strategy.

Questions to consider:

- What core natural skills were you born with that seem to be strengths?

- What values in your life were instilled on you by someone else?

- What values did you seem to develop naturally on your own along the way?

- Were you taught any lessons when you were younger that you had to *unlearn* as you got older?

3

The Game Board

The "Game Board" is a representation of our unique life in front of us. Just like a normal board game or fantasy type adventure game, our real-world life is filled with a series of objectives, obstacles, and goals to achieve.

So, let's try to analyze what we're up against. Try to get a sense of this game board of life and see what the goals are and what kind of obstacles we may find. It's necessary to find out what our character will be up against so we can at least try to prepare and train ourselves as much as possible. And just like any other game we play, of course we want to 'win'.

Ok, so if you want to be good at life and "succeed", here is a short list of all the things you will need to do according to scientific research, life experts, motivational speakers, family, and friends.

Health / Hygiene:
1. Eat a balanced breakfast every morning
2. Exercise with an elevated heart rate for at least 30 minutes every day
3. Brush your teeth and floss at least twice a day
4. Drink 6-8 glasses of water
5. Get at least 8 hours of sleep
6. Avoid sugar, junk food, and high cholesterol items
7. Eliminate bad habits
8. Reduce screen time
9. Measure and watch your weight
10. Avoid too much alcohol
11. Stretch regularly to increase physical flexibility
12. Don't smoke
13. Only eat whole foods, no processed or packaged items
14. Meditate every morning
15. Learn how medical insurance and hospital billing systems work
16. Don't have unprotected sex
17. Get regular checkups with your family doctor
18. Eliminate all harmful addictions
19. Keep a healthy network of good friends for social interactions and mutual support
20. Make time to engage in a hobby, sport, music, art, or other personal interest
21. Take care of your mental health and avoid stressful situations like this list

Profession / Work:
1. Always be on time
2. Go above and beyond
3. Never procrastinate
4. Set goals for yourself
5. Always look professional, dress for success

6. Continue your education by taking night classes to expand your skills and career
7. Expand your professional network and contacts
8. Save for retirement
9. Never be late for meetings
10. Have perfect punctuation and grammar in all your emails and correspondence
11. Smile and act professionally at all times
12. Always exceed the expectations of customers and clients

Friends / Community:
1. Be active in local fundraisers
2. Volunteer for opportunities like garbage cleanups and charity events
3. Cook meals for the homeless or a sick friend
4. Make time to listen when your friends are suffering and in need
5. Be educated about local politics so you can be an informed and responsible voter
6. Recycle your garbage correctly
7. Attend city council meetings so you can be involved in improving your local community
8. Be considerate and polite to both neighbors and strangers

Home:
1. Wash the floors once a week
2. Establish a personal budget and stick to it
3. Keep up with the yardwork
4. Do laundry
5. Perform regular maintenance of your vehicle(s)
6. Keep an emergency fund for unexpected home repairs

7. Learn handyman skills so you can do your own plumbing, carpentry, and electrical work to save money.
8. Wash dishes
9. Do more laundry
10. Water the plants
11. Shop for groceries (Only good deals and always use coupons!!)
12. Vacuum and dust regularly
13. Make sure you always have a better garden than your neighbor
14. Keep the counters clean
15. Take out the garbage, but compost what you can
16. Change your bedsheets weekly
17. Keep up with the latest trends by decorating your home with the correct furniture, pictures, and centerpiece arrangements. Be minimalist yet modern!
18. Take care of any pets (feed, water, train, clean, walk, take to the vet)

Family:
1. Call your parents at least once a week
2. Respect your elderly relatives by calling and visiting them regularly
3. Be available for emergencies and support when needed
4. Care for them when nobody else will; full time if necessary.

If you have a spouse:
1. Take time out of your schedule to nurture your relationship. (Regular vacations or relationship retreats)
2. Learn their love language so you can connect with their needs instead of what you *think* they should want

3. Take actions or restraints to accommodate their emotional needs
4. Always treat them with the utmost respect and cooperation
5. Work as a team so you can tackle life by looking in the same direction rather than at each other
6. Avoid being selfish and always try to do more for your partner than they do for you
7. Make them feel special at all holidays, functions, and special occasions
8. Communicate and be honest at all times
9. Never do that thing you're not supposed to do

If you have kids: (Oh boy, here we go…)
1. Baby proof your house for safety
2. Learn first aid
3. Always give them the best nutrition, especially infants
4. Make sure they follow a regular sleep schedule
5. Teach them how to read (1,000 books before kindergarten)
6. Get them ready for school every day
7. Help them with their homework and monitor their grades
8. Communicate with their teachers regularly about their behavior and progress
9. Monitor their social media posts
10. Set up protected Wi-Fi and lock devices if necessary
11. Teach them good values
12. Limit screen time
13. Teach them good manners and how to behave at special events or services
14. Be involved with their sports and activities
15. Buy birthday presents and coordinate parties for them and their friends
16. Teach them how to swim and ride a bike

17. Keep them away from porn, sex, and drugs at all costs
18. Train them to be respectful to others, but also confident to have independent thoughts and feelings
19. Set a good example with all your words and actions
20. Discipline responsibly and consistently
21. Teach the boys how to take care of a girl
22. Teach the girls how to take care of themselves
23. Be aware of who their friends are and who they are spending time with
24. Encourage creative activities like art, music, and drama
25. Buy just the right amount and the right kind of Christmas presents
26. Set boundaries while teaching them responsibility
27. Set a good example, because they are watching you at all times
28. Communicate with their friends' parents so you can coordinate to keep them safe
29. Teach them about budgeting and financial responsibilities
30. Sit down at a family dinner together every night
31. Be inspirational and motivational whenever you can
32. Teach them HOW to think, not WHAT to think
33. Involve them in household chores and shared responsibilities
34. Teach them all the life lessons you wish you knew as a child
35. Teach them how to drive
36. Take care of them when they are sick
37. Stick up for them when they are falsely accused
38. Understand their individual emotional and physical needs for proper social development

39. Dodge the heartbreaks when they scream how much they hate you and call you a pathetic loser.

If you are part of the Evangelical Christian Faith:
1. Take time out to pray and read scripture every day
2. Look for opportunities to serve the church family
3. Tithe with your finances
4. Commit your life to spreading the gospel to save others
5. Always do the right thing and become a worthy ambassador of the church
6. Be ready to become a martyr if needed
7. Remember the sermon that life is not about what you want, but what God wants
8. Make sure everything you do during the day is motivated by the glory of God
9. Be pure in spirit and never compromise any moral boundaries
10. Remember all the things that you SHOULD be doing right now to please the Lord
11. Try to be good at all times in all ways
12. Raise your children to follow the same beliefs and values
13. Love your neighbor. (Yes, including *that* one.)

This is of course a funny list, but then again it's not funny at all. All the items on this list are really good things to do that we can't argue against. So, of course we try to do them all! And it doesn't take long to find hundreds more. But it's not often that we get a chance to step back and look at a list like this and actually reflect on how truly ridiculous it is. It's really no wonder we're exhausted and overwhelmed.

And there's more! In a society of hyper capitalism, you are no longer born as a person but as a potential customer. So, it's no accident that you feel compelled to continuously buy and consume something. You are compelled to work to earn more money to consume more things. And in the information age, you and your data are essentially now the product, just waiting to be sold to someone else so it's easier for *them* to sell you something.

Also, don't forget about all the pop-up ads, commercials, news outlets, and social media blurbs that are specifically designed to make you engaged and depressed. Companies purposefully employ behavioral psychologists that use very specific techniques to make you miserable unless you click on something and add it to the shopping cart. It's not possible to escape, and they're getting EXTREMELY good at it.

Now mix this in with the values and priorities that were instilled on us by society, parents, or someone else. There are so many priorities thrown at us that we can't even think straight. It's like fighting a war and getting ambushed on all fronts.

Know Your Character, Know The Challenges

The point of all this is to begin to identify exactly what we are facing. These are the bears and ghosts that your random dice-created character will be fighting against during your adventure here on this planet. Many of us have unwillingly migrated to a position of just surviving, let alone thriving and succeeding.

Given this foundation, depending on what your original dice roll was, some obstacles will be easy for you. Others maybe not so much. Some challenges are right in front of your face. Others won't apply or you may not even be aware of them.

We often make the mistake of trying to compare ourselves with someone else. But because of all these dice rolls we're dealing with, every one of us is essentially playing on a different game board using a different character with different abilities. When you truly understand this analogy, it becomes ridiculous to measure yourself against the progress or situation of someone else.

Again, the key point here is that the difficulty of the challenges you decide to tackle are NOT THE SAME for everyone. All those core traits that you didn't have a choice about will absolutely start to make a difference here.

How Your Dice Rolls Can Affect Your Progress

Here are a few examples of how those initial dice rolls can directly affect your ability to upgrade your character:

Exercise for at least 30 minutes every day:
Exercising has enormous benefits for us both physically and mentally. Feeling good physically allows you to learn better, to let your body function better, to accomplish more during the day, and to just feel better all around. That immediately puts you into a much better position to achieve other skill upgrades! Again, that's exactly why exercise is usually a key foundation of almost all those recommended self-help routines.

Let's say you rolled a 5 on the athletic dice. Your parents probably encouraged you to play sports in school, so developing the habit to exercise daily might come VERY easily for you. It may already be a natural habit and jogging 5 miles a day is almost effortless and no problem!!

But for someone who rolled a 1 in the athletic department, this one simple habit could be a much more difficult mountain to climb. Maybe it wasn't your fault that exercising and engaging in sports simply weren't a part of your life growing up. Maybe you weren't allowed to play sports or couldn't for whatever reason. Hopefully you can see how rolling a 5 or 6 can put you at a huge advantage in upgrading your initial position here. Not only for the obvious health reasons, but also to point you onto the direct path for learning other skills.

Quitting an addiction:

Because of differences in brain chemistry, hormones, and hereditary genetics, people often make the mistake of thinking all addiction recoveries should have the same result if they would just put in the same effort. Many people think that if recovery didn't work for you, then you obviously didn't want to get better or just didn't try hard enough. But someone who has a heavy genetic disposition of addiction is facing a much different challenge than someone who maybe just picked up a bad habit. Our brains are a flowing chaotic soup of sometimes unpredictable chemicals and cognitive abilities. Remember it's a range of factors and intensities, not a binary situation. If you've struggled personally with this, you know how frustrating it can be to witness how someone else can seem to recover so easily while you're barely making any progress. It can be exhausting and disheartening to watch other people succeed while you continue to struggle.

But remember that everyone is starting from a unique position under a unique situation. The dice may have given you different size baggage to carry up a much bigger mountain. That isn't necessarily your fault. Don't think for a minute that you can't do it. But it's critical to acknowledge that the underlying difficulty of the task may require more creative approaches or tenacity. Sometimes it's comforting to know that there IS a light at the end of your tunnel, but unfortunately your tunnel may be a bit longer and may have a few more curves.

Reading/Learning:
Reading and education are certainly one of the biggest keys to upgrading areas of your life. You can soak in more information, learn more skills, learn how to learn. But for someone with dyslexia, a visual handicap, or a learning disorder, those bad dice immediately become a HUGE disadvantage. Someone combatting these or other challenges like this will use an enormous amount of time and energy just trying to achieve the one core skill that can open the doors of knowledge for so many other skills.

The entire point here is that some people are naturally better equipped to handle certain challenges more efficiently than others. Not everyone has the same capacity, strength, or energy levels. People are playing this game with different characters, and we MUST acknowledge that.

We Need To Possess A Variety Of Skills Against A Variety Of Challenges

Another key detail to see from any list of skills and goals is that it takes a variety of different skill sets to successfully accomplish them. Examples:
- Having a solid work ethic is critical to performing well at your job

- Being compassionate and caring is important for managing the well-being of a child
- Being frugal and disciplined is important for your financial success
- Having good social skills is vital for being active and engaged in the community
- Having good leadership skills is necessary for management and setting a good example to others
- Developing good habits in hygiene and self-care is important for how you look and present yourself to others
- Having a good self-esteem is important to give you confidence in your abilities and more independence in your decision making.
- Having good manners and respect for others is essential for social interactions and networking.

"Life is like a box of chocolates; you never know what you're going to get." - Forrest Gump

That's a classic movie line that we all smile at and agree with. But why do we often forget to apply it to our own lives?

The real problem we face is that not all of us rolled 6s in all these categories. Therefore, we must pick and choose which skills we want to focus on to improve and upgrade for the best results. It's just not realistic or reasonable to expect that we can be the best at everything we take on. So, it's our values that help us determine what those most important skills are and what we decide to upgrade.

Therein lies the challenge! Again, everyone has different values because of all these dice flying around everywhere. Is it money? Relationships? Serving the community? Music or art? Having a good work ethic? Compassion for others? Education? Parenting? Having a clean house? Physical appearance?

We have no idea what monsters or treasures the gameboard of life will throw at us. All we can do is the best we can to prepare for whatever comes our way. Some of us will succeed but many will not.

Questions to consider:

- What does your life game board look like?

- What life challenges have you personally decided to take on? Which are you avoiding?

- Do you notice that some challenges seem to be more difficult for you to accomplish compared to someone else? Do you notice any that might be easier for you than others?

- When you look at your game board, do you adjust your game strategy based on the natural skills of your character?

4

Upgrades

Upgrades are when something happens to us that allows us to start throwing dice which give us a greater probability of success. It's when we increase our number roll for any given skill or ability that we are fundamentally able to. Upgrades can come in the form of learning a new skill, increasing the dice value of a naturally existing trait or skill, or simply increasing the probability of something good happening to us. Skills from the dice are everything.

Types Of Skills

Examples of hard external skills:
- Learning to swim
- Learning to cook
- Learning a trade like carpentry, welding, or gardening
- Become comfortable and accomplished with public speaking

Examples of softer internal skills:
- Finding compassion for others
- Being responsible and dependable
- Patience
- Generosity

Again, one of the great challenges of this life is that we have no idea what dice rolls we got. Part of the fun (and frustration) is trying to figure out what those dice are and what numbers we may have started with. Because of the random distribution of how the dice work, it's very likely we're probably good at some skills, but not so much with others. There are thousands of variables and possibilities of abilities of which we're probably not even aware of. Making an effort to learn new skills helps us sort that out.

Throw As Many Dice As You Can

It's critical to our mental health and fitness that our bodies engage in something that they were biologically meant to do. These are the activities we generally like to do or seem naturally gifted at. One of the many benefits of learning as many new skills as possible is to find out exactly what those natural gifts are. Most of us are usually fairly hesitant to try new things, but it's the only way to learn more about ourselves and to find out what we truly enjoy doing. So, whenever we attempt to learn a new skill, we are essentially throwing more dice on the table. And because of math, that immediately gives us more chances to hit a big number.

Learning a new skill often has the added benefit of making many things in your life a bit easier. In the examples above, learning how to cook is a great way to save money and encourage healthy eating for your friends and family. Learning how to fix a sink or change a car tire can come in handy when you need it. Being patient allows you to wait for something with much less anguish. Skills almost always build on each other, setting you up for even more chances for success in other areas. Also, new skills may often lead to a new source of income or career.

Once we figure out what we do well or things we enjoy doing, it's important for us to push it and see how much we can get out of it. Why is that? When someone is naturally good at something, that automatically gives them a distinct advantage with anything else related to that area. It means they will be able to perform and improve at that distinct skill more quickly than other people. Think of this as kind of like a bonus; and a key strategy in almost every game is to always take advantage of bonuses!

Let's look at a couple situations:
For example, consider someone who is naturally good at math. Maybe they were born with a 5 in that skill and math related classes in school were always a breeze for them. They have the potential to learn how to process advanced equations and calculus very quickly. The better at math they get, the better they get at anything else *related* to math. That opens the door for other skills and possible job opportunities like accounting, statistics, or economics. They would certainly have more success on those paths rather than something like nursing or acting.

Another example is someone who may be creative and likes to work with their hands. Sitting in an office might put them at a disadvantage on that path. But they could excel at a job that requires building or fixing things with their hands like a carpenter or mechanic. The better you are at your job, the easier it becomes. Therefore, if you happen to have a natural ability that supports a given career, that career will be easier for you than it is for someone else with less abilities in that same position. Not that a mechanic couldn't work in an office if they wanted to, but it could turn out to be a much more difficult road. Remember, it's important to really get to know the character with which you have to play the game. Then develop a game strategy that best matches your character.

If your true passion unfortunately can't be your career, at least take it up as a hobby so you can feed that hungry part of your biology.

Increasing Probabilities With Core Base Skills

Another key life hack for upgrading ourselves is to increase the probabilities that something good will happen to us. We can't have the attitude that good things are only reserved for the people that started out with all 6s. There are so many underlying reasons why changing your luck is possible and how this works.

That's essentially the goal of this entire journey. We can never guarantee our success. But we can at least try to set ourselves up for the best possible odds to succeed.

Education is probably the most obvious example here. Education gives you a base skill to unlock so many other skill sets. It's also unique because it is something that can't be taken away from you. I'm not just talking about staying in school to get a job. I'm talking about learning as much as you can in as many areas as you can. Again, skills often compound on each other. The more skills you learn, the easier learning other skills can become. You start to see patterns in the world. You may learn key concepts and foundations that are used as building blocks to understand more complicated realities. You increase your perspective on many topics, which gives you a better chance at making good decisions. Making good decisions directly increases your chances of succeeding in whatever you are doing.

That's why learning to read is such a fundamentally important skill to master while we are young. It's an essential building block that allows direct access to so many others. It's basically the difference between using a straw and using a vacuum cleaner to suck up potential.

Mental and physical health are also way up there in terms of simple base skills that can be foundational for so many others. Having your body in the best possible condition sets it up to function much more efficiently. A better functioning body will think and feel better. A boost of energy to accomplish more during the day. Clearer thinking that will lead to better decision making. Better sleep. Better mood. Better almost everything. Again, that's exactly why exercise and meditation are such highly recommended daily habits for so many self-improvement techniques and therapies. They are foundational in creating a solid base for adding and upgrading almost every other skill.

Who you spend your time with is another highly recommended good habit. Remember that we learn our worldview from our surroundings and the people we are close to whether we realize it or not. It stands to reason then that we are more likely to pick up good habits and skills from people that we admire and want to emulate. Our bodies instinctively start to imitate the attitudes and habits of the people around us. It literally changes our brain chemistry and causes us to function in a more positive and healthier environment. That's something we CAN directly control and why choosing the people you hang out with is another key recommendation by many of those self-help books. We often want our kids to stay away from bad influences, but how often do we take that same advice?

There are so many other examples. Making some simple wise decisions about our daily habits and behaviors absolutely helps our chances of something good happening to us. Even small things become important like having good manners and being polite. Those types of behaviors are critical in establishing good communication and positive interactions with other people. Those interactions will in turn lead to more opportunities for success.

Because of the chaotic results of the dice, sometimes it does take luck. But it's important we have the skills to take advantage of any luck when we get it.

Upgrade Examples:

Let's look at some basic examples of what it means to upgrade some simple skills. These are some basic skills that should all be familiar to all of us so we can start to visualize the different levels and progression. We'll use a standard 6-sided die; the number will indicate your skill level based on a progressive range of expertise.

Skill: Keyboard Typing
Related Skills: Dexterity, Hand-Eye Coordination

1 = Takes you a few moments to scan the keyboard and poke a key one at a time with your index finger.
2 = You know about where the keys are, but you still have to poke at them. Maybe with two fingers.
3 = You use all your fingers in the correct position but still have to look at the keyboard most of the time.
4 = You can type efficiently without looking

5 = You can type with accelerated speed about 70 words per minute
6 = You have fully mastered the keyboard with an accurate rate and speeds over 90+ words per minute

Typing is a skill that should be familiar to most everyone so hopefully you can relate to this progression at least in some way. From your observation of watching friends learn how to type, you may notice that many people will progress through some of these levels faster than others. That's where the related skills may come in, meaning that someone who has very good dexterity and coordination will probably progress much more quickly than somebody who is clumsy and "all thumbs". You may also notice that you probably need to have excellent levels in those other base abilities to even make it to level 6. Some people can practice all they want, but they may never be able to get past level 5, but most everyone should be able to get to a 3 or 4 with at least some time and effort.

Keyboard typing is also an excellent example of a core skill that leads to yet other skills. It increases productivity if you do any type of work on a computer. You can write blogs, emails, or articles with much less time and effort. It directly improves correspondence and communication with other people. It's a great example of a skill that is used to build others.

Skill: Listening
Related Skills: Patience, Presence/Focus

1 = You rarely even acknowledge someone is talking to you. Completely distracted.
2 = You hear some of their words, but your mind is elsewhere and you're not truly paying attention.

3 = You hear most of their words and are at least trying to pay attention to what they are saying.
4 = You are looking directly at them and hearing everything they are saying. But your mind keeps wandering a bit and you're not totally focused.
5 = You hear what they are saying, understand most of it, but are eager to quickly jump in with your own thoughts and opinions.
6 = Totally engaged. You give them your full attention in both focus and presence. You can repeat everything they say and let it fully sink in before you respond or act.

This skill is a little softer and more abstract. The levels with softer skills are a bit harder to define but hopefully you can still see some sort of a progression. To upgrade and improve on how well you listen to someone, you probably need a good foundation of any related skills like focus and patience. Maybe even empathy. That also infers that the simple skill of listening may be inherently very difficult for some people depending on those other skills. Do you value listening to someone else during all personal interactions? How much you value other people in general may determine how much effort you put into your listening skills.

Most, if not all, skills require at least some level of experience or expertise, and it's a great exercise to think about skills like these and define some sort of ranked progression. With that in mind, it's best to think of upgrading as leveling yourself up through those progressions. And when upgrading, always be mindful of other related skills may be helpful or necessary while navigating through the upgrade process.

Downgrades

It goes without saying that we should also avoid downgrades. These are anything that would negatively impact our positive life probabilities. If it's possible, we need to avoid situations that may carry extreme risk or even cause permanent damage.

Some obvious examples:
- Drug/Alcohol abuse
- Teen pregnancy
- Gangs or unnecessary violence
- Criminal activity
- Negative or abusive influences

Every parent knows those kinds of things can be a showstopper which is why they are such a big deal on the child-raising radar. They are the exact reason why agencies like the FCC (Federal Communications Commission) and MPAA (Motion Picture Association) exist and why they have guidelines with rating scales for children and young adults. It's the reason why we need agencies like child protection services and other organizations that are designed to keep children out of harm's way as much as possible. Deep down we all instinctively know that certain adult content and behavior have a direct negative influence on the development of young children. (I would say they even have a dangerous influence on adults, but we often avoid that conversation.) Content like that directly shapes children's worldview in a way that is neither healthy nor safe. Those negative influences can directly downgrade their life probabilities. We can't always prevent bad things from happening to children or ourselves. But we should at least try to avoid them as much as possible.

Life is hard enough. It is NOT a good game strategy to make it any more difficult than it already is.

The worst bane of many downgrades is that they unfortunately can have a direct negative effect on other people around us. Problems like drug and alcohol abuse or teen pregnancy certainly affect the lives of family members, friends, and relatives. It's one thing to downgrade yourself, but it's never fair to cripple the innocent when it can be avoided.

Maximize Your Probability

There's actually no requirement to do any of this. You always have the option of just sitting back and living with what you got, but the casino game of life makes it hard to get a win no matter what you do. It's up to us to make the best decisions we can to upgrade our chances of success in whatever challenge is given to us by whatever enemy we may face.

Remember the goal is never to guarantee success, but only to maximize your probabilities of hopefully beating that ghost. Choose your values wisely, and then upgrade the skills you need so you can start rolling with the highest numbers possible.

Questions to consider:

- What upgrades have you worked on in your life that you can celebrate?

- What bad habits have you picked up that you know are affecting your probabilities for success?

- What skills can you identify that create a good foundation to facilitate learning and mastering other skills?

5

Number Bias

Number Bias is the natural tendency for us to think people rolled the same numbers we did.

It comes in many forms including common prejudice or just the general assumptions we tend to make about other people and their abilities. But it can also come from a desire to believe that other people *should* have the same values and skill sets that we do, or that they *should* get the same results for their efforts if they execute the exact same steps that we did.

We refer to the collection of our unique experiences and perspectives as our own personal worldview. It's the total accumulation of our core attributes, abilities, and circumstances that create the perceived reality of the world we live in. We are continually being influenced by our parents, friends, strangers, community, natural abilities, and life circumstances. With so many combinations, it's not possible for anyone else to see and experience the world exactly the same way we do.

Cliques And Social Preferences

High School serves as a fantastic laboratory for some observations. One of the universal things that seems to happen in adolescence is the formation of local friend groups that we call cliques. Do you notice that almost every single teen movie is full of them? The jocks, the nerds, the burnouts, the cheerleaders, the goths, etc.: groups of kids that fit into a similar profile that many of us can identify from experience. There's a good chance we can relate to some of them in one way or another.

Why are these cliques such a standard concept that everyone seems to understand? I believe most cliques form naturally because of the subtle gravitation of wanting to be with other people that are just like us. We instinctively want to spend time with other people who share similar skills, goals, and experiences. Other people who may have had similar dice rolls and who probably view the world in the same way we do. They share common successes or maybe have had similar painful experiences. They probably have the same interests and values. These similar worldviews become almost like a shared common language, making communication and cooperation so much easier between people that may natively share these underlying qualities. They seem to understand each other without even talking about it. They would in turn share similar values or motivations. People who don't share these core traits wouldn't easily understand them and are therefore kept out.

Do we think any of this magically stops after high school? It's very naive to think so. I think one of the biggest traps we fall into even as adults is that we tend to think that everyone should view and react to the world the same way we do. After all, we know what's best and true from our own personal experience and values. We have direct personal evidence to support it! Unfortunately, we can only view the world from our eyes. I like to think of this trap as something called Number Bias; expecting everyone else to view and interact with the world from the perspective of our own set of dice. It's unfortunate that so many people refuse to acknowledge different perspectives and at least spend some minimal effort trying to understand them. They either simply don't want to or may lack the physical ability.

Perspective Of What You See

Here's a simple exercise to help visualize the point:
Imagine a huge rectangular block about the size of a house laying on its side. One person is standing in front of the block, and another is standing to directly to the side of the block. The first person looks at the object and can only see a rectangle. The other person is standing from a vantage point where they can only see a square. They begin to argue about what the object is and who is right. Maybe they start shouting about it on Twitter or Facebook? They grab their friends who happen to be standing right next to them and they agree!! See! You're wrong! It's a square!!! They start shouting and arguing to the death because everything they can observe and experience about this object proves them to be right. They of course believe in the truth! It never once occurs to them that they could both be wrong.

The best way to have an argument with someone is to understand your opponent's position better than they do. I often wonder how many times activists and politicians take the time to do that.

Ranchers vs The City

My kids won't hesitate to tell you that I often look for new and devious ways to torture them. So, in the summer of 2017, I stuffed them into a minivan, and we headed off for the traditional family trip out west. The trip involved thousands of miles on the road driving across 17 states in 14 days. Heading east to west across the plains, over the mountains, and of course the traditional side detours to the famous Corn Palace and Wall Drug. You don't realize how big this country is until you try to drive across it. It's awe inspiring to think people once walked across it!

In any case, while we were seemingly lost somewhere in Wyoming, it really struck me where we were and who lived here. It was a great opportunity to see the world from a completely different perspective. Nothing but cattle ranchers, true cowboys, and a bunch of wide-open spaces for miles and miles. I took a serious moment to focus on how different the lives of these people are compared to the citizens of a concrete jungle in any given metropolitan city. It was a very inspiring moment for me to try to visualize the results of these different dice rolls. These ranchers looked out of their window only to see acres and acres of plains and maybe a few mountains 70 miles away. Their closest neighbor could have been 15 miles away. City dwellers enjoy scenery of majestic buildings, exciting lights, and occasional honking car horns. City neighbors may only be a few feet away from each other at all times.

The odd burning question that stuck in my head was how is it possible for a centralized governing body to create rules and laws that would even remotely apply to both these groups of people? The only thing they might have in common is hair color. They experience completely opposite environments, lifestyles, history, values, experiences, and worldviews. Of course, this would include a completely different set of problems and solutions that a shared government could possibly be of any help to address.

I always try to make it a point to avoid getting political. Nothing good usually comes of it and our current political situation has become unbelievably frustrating. But in light of understanding the principles about how and why people can view the world so differently, I think the great taboo barrier of politics is a great illustration of a kind of number bias. It makes it a bit easier to understand why there is a problem.

Whether we like it or not, we are directly influenced by our environment and the people with whom we interact. Plenty of research confirms this. Our peers help shape our opinions. They impact us morally, intellectually, and philosophically. This usually comes in the form of a church, family, friends, or social club. People usually join a political party because they are naturally attracted to the same values and beliefs as the leaders. I don't think it's a coincidence that people who happen to live in the same environments with the same influences usually end up with the same political affiliation. Of course, there are always exceptions. But generally speaking, I think the political geographical map shows this trend pretty well. That famous blue/red map of the United States clearly tells us that where you live appears to make a huge difference in what you may believe politically. We think it shouldn't, but it plainly does.

I know several people who have changed political parties after they moved to a different part of the country. How can that be if there is only one "truth" as our leaders say? Perhaps simply viewing life from a different perspective

can cause people to completely change their opinion on many of the issues we face?
If you were brainwashed, would you know it?

Who Is In Front Of You?

As a kid, I spent my summers growing up on the shore of Chautauqua Lake in western New York state. Within the famous Institution there is a world renown community known for its collaboration of music, art, education, and philosophy. Every summer season, they have a feast of cultural events, classes, and entertainment fueled by prestigious guests and speakers from all over the world. It's something you don't really appreciate as a kid, but it was a gold mine for summer jobs.

One of my jobs for a few summers was to work on the stage crew of the central concert hall that we call the Amphitheater. We would set the stage up for a guest speaker in the morning, lay the dance floor for ballet practice in the afternoon, and then set up for whatever big show was scheduled for that evening. Every day was something different depending on the schedule.

There is a full-scale symphony orchestra that plays a few nights a week at the Amphitheater which is composed of some of the best musicians in the country. Symphony nights are generally pretty boring for us kids, so the stage crew members usually hide in our little cubby hole office trying to find ways to quietly entertain ourselves during the show. We were on a card game kick that month and were looking for a fourth player for a game called Euchre. Some raggedy older gentleman was walking by our table, noticed our dilemma, and asked if he could play. It was very normal for people to come and go during the bustle of the show, so we didn't really think anything of it. We of course were happy to oblige and got right into it.

If you know anything about the exotic card game of Euchre, it's not really a game that makes any sense at first. The actual fun mostly has nothing to do with the cards and is more about the trash talking against the other players. The real object of the game is to throw down winning trump cards while trying to come up with the best insult you can against your opponents. This weird guy we just picked up of course knew that, so it didn't take long for us to engage in some heavy verbal combat. He started making fun of our uniforms, and I think we responded with comments about his hair or something he was wearing. We noticed he had a bit of an English accent so that gave us ammunition to start making fun of the queen or something related to tea time. He laughed and laughed as we took turns slapping down cards and had a fantastic time.

After several minutes, he paused in the middle of a hand as he heard something in the background. He set down his cards and said: "Oh no sorry, I have to go!". He then proceeded to sprint down the hallway, round the corner, and step out directly onto the stage. Mind you this was in the middle of the performance in front of a crowd of about 6,000 people. As it turns out, he was the guest conductor for the evening, and we had absolutely no idea. After an initial barrage of fierce clapping, he immediately proceeded to command a 65-person orchestra for a full non-stop 20-minute piece completely from memory. He used no sheet music because he had memorized every single note for each instrument for the entire 20-minute performance. There are only a handful of people in the world who have the ability to do this. The crowd cheered, thunderous applause. He walked off the stage and directly back to our little office. He picked up his cards, apologized for the delay, and asked if we could start playing again.

This raggedy disheveled gentleman was one of the principal conductors of the world-renowned London Symphony Orchestra, and he was sitting right in front of us trying to figure out the best way to make fun of our mothers.

It's a great story and always a reminder to me that we never know who may be standing right in front of us. We never know what bag of dice they may be holding in their pocket. What journey did they have to take to get there? What hidden skills do they have? What events have they experienced in their life that helped shape who they are? What is their unique perspective on this life we are living? What obstacles have they had to climb over and step through? What dice did they roll? Number bias inherently forces us to make so many assumptions. And sometimes it often causes us to miss so much.

Number Bias and Relationships

Number bias can also absolutely have an unseen effect on our relationships and how we interact with other people. Because of how we see the world, we often don't take into account how other people mentally operate and what their inherent needs are. (If we're even aware of and acknowledge those differences in the first place.)

Let's look at a simple classic example of a relationship between Mary and Susan who are trying very hard to be friends.

The Dice of Life

Situation: Susan is an accountant at a large corporate firm. She's just been reassigned to work in the records department which is located in an isolated hallway in the basement of their main office building. Her new job assignment will be to review and refile several old cases that were archived several years ago. It's a slow task that requires some time and patience, so it looks like she'll be stuck down there for quite a while. She is not happy!

Susan is very distraught about the whole situation and needs some support. She calls her friend Mary for help. Being the good friend that she is, Mary is of course very eager to help and comes right over. "Here, I made a card for you and baked you some muffins. I thought you may like this book I just read about meditating in nature. It's really good, and it teaches you how to slow down and reflect on your inner self. I really think it can help you in this tough time."

Situation: Mary is a graphic designer at a marketing firm. Her company just landed a new client, and her team is scrambling to get ready. They're already planning several extra meetings, brainstorming sessions, and after-hour social meetups to get to know the new client and their needs. She feels overwhelmed.

Mary is of course stressed out and calls her friend Susan for help. In turn, Susan is excited to return the favor and help support her friend. "You definitely need to get out!" Susan exclaims. "I'll call the rest of the girls and we'll take you out to dinner. Then we'll all go out for drinks after and have a great time. Believe me! That's totally what you need to make you feel better!"

Now before we start making any assumptions about who gave the best response here, let's learn a bit more about Mary and Susan. We're trying to avoid number bias here so it's critical to look at what kind of people they are and see what kind of dice they may be holding in their bag.

Mary is inherently a very shy and quiet person. A classic introvert. Sometimes she doesn't mind being around people, but she is usually most comfortable just listening or being an observer.

Susan on the other hand, is an extrovert who is very outgoing, outspoken, and loves to be around people for a good time. She's a talker with high energy and going to parties totally excites her.

Now after knowing that information, it becomes obvious to see that the solution they provided to each other is exactly NOT what should have been done. Both Mary and Susan gave the advice that they themselves would have *wanted*. They did NOT take into account what the other person actually *needed*. So, because of their own personal experience and worldview, they just assumed that whatever makes *them* feel better is exactly what the other person would want as well. They essentially have a number bias and it's affecting their ability to relate to each other. We see this happen in relationships all the time and it's a direct result of people not having the simple understanding that people threw different dice. Of course we know people are different, yet we continually forget to apply it in our real life relationships with each other. All too often we impose our own expectations and desires onto someone else.

But wait, there's actually so much more going on here. Now that we know what kind of people Mary and Susan are, let's take a deeper look at their situations again.

Susan is an outgoing, energetic person who was just placed into an environment where there will be no people around. She'll essentially be isolated in the basement with little contact and no interactions with anyone else for quite some time. This new assignment at work is going directly against Susan's character as a person and is the actual underlying reason for her stress. Mary certainly understands that Susan is upset. But it doesn't even occur to Mary WHY Susan would be bothered by that situation. Mary would probably love that same job assignment and think nothing of it.

Mary on the other hand, is being placed into situations that are going to be very social forcing her to get out of her comfort zone. It doesn't even register to Susan how difficult that will be for Mary to go through. She wants to help Mary, but Susan can't truly relate to the actual problem or even see it. What Mary is experiencing would just be another day in Susan's world. Susan doesn't think twice that it would be stressful to anyone to be put into the simple situation of being around other people.

This is a simple example but, hopefully, it illustrates the deeper point very well. It's not that we don't *want* to understand something about someone, but because of our own dice roll and worldview, we actually may lack the social, emotional, mental, or even physical ability. We often quickly blame people for not understanding something about us. Of course, it can get very frustrating when sometimes they just don't get it, but do we ever forgive them because they simply can't?

Now, factor in the more complicated dice rolls of ethics, morality, empathy, and values. This leads us to one of the most important conundrums of number bias and the entire underlying concept of this dice analogy:

Not only do we apply our own unique solutions to many of the problems we see, but we have a completely different understanding of what the problems actually are in the first place.

Number Fixedness

Number bias can of course take many other forms that we may not realize. There's another dimension of this that can only be described as number fixedness. That's the phenomenon that once we learn something about someone, we tend to think they always were, and always will be at that same number.

Number fixedness is the core reason why first impressions are so important. As most of us know, once somebody makes up their mind about something, it's actually hard work to change it. So, a first impression is exactly what sets that stage. It's also the reason why someone's reputation may be so important. For some reason, it only takes a few short sentences or rumors about a person to cause us to lock them into a box possibly for the rest of their life. We seem to always remember that one thing that we heard or saw from a person 15 years ago.

For our own sake, we absolutely must believe that it's possible for people to change. We thrive in the hope that we can learn, improve, and upgrade ourselves, so why is it so hard for us to believe that other people may evolve and change from what they once were as well?

If you spend a lot of time together with someone, maybe even a friend or family member, you start to know that person REALLY well. Maybe you know their patterns, their preferences, and their habits. You may even be able to predict what they'll say or do. But once in a while they may surprise you. They may do something unexpected or react in a way you didn't anticipate. Did something change?

My wife and I have been together for over 20 years and we still continue to surprise each other all the time with this. We've gone through so many life challenges together that we had an opportunity to learn many of the same life lessons together. During those struggles and trials, our values and understanding of the world have absolutely changed along the way. The world didn't change, but only our perspective. After living through so many life experiences, things that were once black and white are no longer so obvious. Parenting taught us that we actually knew nothing about kids and how people work. We learned that our parents weren't always right about everything. We are absolutely NOT the same people we were 20 years ago. Are you?

Number Bias And Gameboards

With the dice directly affecting our perspectives and opinions, it's also naïve to think the dice create the same overall life 'gameboards' for everyone else. Imagine two random 10-year-old boys. One boy is raised in a wealthy safe neighborhood, while the other boy grows up in the ghetto of the inner city. The first boy spends his Saturday mornings at the Country Club learning the proper etiquette around the putting green. In his world, that will be an important skill for him to master to help him succeed on the gameboard that lies in front of him. The other boy learns how to dodge the police and how to protect himself during a drive-by shooting. Very different skills will be needed and valued by each of them to succeed in much different life adventures. They will be taught at a young age to have very different goals and objectives. They will have a completely different perspective and understanding of how the world works and what needs to be accomplished. As they grow up, it's interesting to think about what advice they would give to each other. Do you think either of them has any authority to understand their situation and know what's best for the other? The same skills and life lessons would not even remotely apply to such different gameboards. It's so easy for us to dish out advice to other people who live in situations we know nothing about. Gameboard Bias sounds like another pitfall we need to avoid.

Questions to consider:

- Are you mentally mature enough to grasp the concept of a different perspective?

- When have you experienced number bias toward someone else?

- When has someone shown number bias against you?

- Have you ever met someone that you know would simply NOT understand your position on something? No matter how hard you try to explain?

- Have you ever heard an argument when two people can't even agree on what the problem is?

- What experience do you have with number fixedness? In yourself? With others?

6

Life Isn't Fair

As a father, I have a series of what my kids call "catch phrases". A few simple words or pieces of advice that I would repeat over and over until they got sick of them. I would walk around the house spouting these phrases and then always pull them out when the time was right. Just little lessons that I found to be helpful in my own personal life that I really wanted my kids to learn as well. They will not hesitate to tell you that "Life Isn't Fair" was near the top of the list. Of course, they would kick and scream every time I said it. But I decided early on that this was an important truth for them to learn.

As much as we hate to come to terms with the idea that life isn't fair, it is absolutely true. Naturally, we want everyone to be treated the same. To have the same opportunities, same outcomes, and same results for the same effort. We can try hard to make everything fair, and we certainly *should* try. But the reality is that we'll never get there. Equal opportunity and equal effort do NOT mean equal results.

The Dice of Life

We all hear the stories about high schools that have 27 valedictorians, or when everyone in a contest gets a trophy. Some of us who are older and maybe a bit wiser tend to snicker at these stories because we know that those kids are in for a huge disappointment later in life. It sets up the expectation that everyone should be a winner in whatever they do. But that's simply not the way the world works no matter how much we wish it were true.

So, the key component of any recovery is acceptance. The sooner we understand this truth, the less it can hurt us.

Here's a typical situation:

Two men work at the same company. Jack shows up to work, does his job well, and goes home. Gary on the other hand shows up to work early every day. He took an extra computer class so he could learn the company's new software system. He constantly asks questions and learns about how the company works and how he can contribute to its success. He makes all the extra efforts, takes on extra assignments, and is happy to stay late when needed. He has a hard work ethic and is doing everything he can to apply it to become a great employee.

One day a management position opens and everyone in the company is encouraged to apply. This is a great career opportunity that they've been waiting for!! Both Jack and Gary immediately apply for the position. Which one of them do you think gets the job??

The correct answer is neither of them. The position went to the Vice President's grandson who just partied for 3 years at college, dropped out, and couldn't find a job anywhere else.

This may be a funny example but it's really not. Situations like this happen all the time and you most likely have several similar stories of your own. People are often granted things they didn't earn or deserve. It skews the true value of hard work and perseverance. We're continually told by motivational speakers that if we work hard, and put in the extra time, that will be the key to success! We get so excited about all the great things that will come to us if we just work hard and believe! Yes, please listen to them. That attitude is absolutely necessary to get there. But the truth here is that the results of our efforts are sometimes dictated by factors that are simply outside of our control. It's not fair.

Ironman

My father-in-law was raised in a relatively poor family with very little resources and expectations. He was a bit of a troublemaker as a kid and could have easily ended up with a much different life than he did. Fortunately, he developed a hard work ethic and made the wise decision early in life to apply himself as much as he could. He learned how to flip houses to save money and put himself through school and became a well-respected CPA. He owned his own accounting firm early in life and became financially successful very quickly. Despite his hard work, the most amazing thing about him was his immense determination of physical fitness: an unbelievable dedication to exercise and physical activities that was nothing less than superhuman. Somehow, he managed to make time for hours of training almost every day. He even competed in the famous Ironman Triathlon which is considered to be one of the most prestigious athletic accomplishments in the world. An Ironman Triathlon constitutes a 2.4 mile swim, a 120 mile bike race, followed by a 26.2 mile marathon. It's hard for some of us mortals to actually get our heads wrapped around that.

Unfortunately, at the age of 48 he was diagnosed with late-stage pancreatic cancer. He was one of the most physically fit and healthiest people on the planet, yet it didn't matter. He died shortly after at the age of 49. He never had a chance to enjoy the efforts of his hard work and financial success in retirement. He never had a chance to take his grandchildren for a bike ride. It devastated his family, friends, and the local sports community. It's not fair.

Unfortunately, most of us have similar stories just like this. There are so many examples of good people dealing with horrible circumstances they don't deserve. Babies that are born with handicaps or terminal diseases. Having to give up a career to stay home and care for a loved one. Traumas and disasters always seem to happen to the nicest people, while we see so many reckless people get all the great breaks and good fortune. It's not fair.

Failure Is Not Always Our Fault

"It is possible to commit no mistakes and still lose. That is not a weakness. That is life."
-Captain Jean-Luc Picard.   Star Trek: The Next Generation

This quote gives me an unbelievable amount of peace and comfort. It's a reminder to me that no matter what decisions I make or how hard I work in life, there is always a chance that I will not succeed. I always remember the randomness of the dice that we're throwing. We must certainly work hard to make good decisions to increase our chances and probabilities, but there is never a guarantee that the outcome will be in our favor.

Failure is not always our fault and I think that's something we need to hear.

Unfair Probabilities

To best understand this concept, it makes sense to look at another popular game called blackjack. Blackjack is a popular casino game that uses a deck of cards that puts you in a heads-up situation against the dealer. The basic objective is to get a higher card total than the dealer getting as close as possible to 21 without going over. Face cards count as 10. Two cards are dealt to yourself, and two cards are dealt to the dealer, with one of the dealer cards face down.

Situation: You are dealt a 5 and a 6 for a current total of 11. The dealer's up card is showing a 6. This is an ideal situation for you. The correct action to take here is to 'hit' and get another card since there is no chance of you busting over 21, and there is a good probability you will get a high card. The card you receive is an 8. That gives you a total of 19, which is not 21, but is still fairly good.

The dealer reveals their second card which is a 4 giving the dealer an original total of 10. The dealer 'hits' again and gets another card which is a Jack. The dealer now has 20 which unfortunately is more than your 19. You lose.

In this situation, you did everything correctly. You did not make a mistake. Your choice of action has the greatest probability of success which is the core strategy of this or any game. But it was still NOT a guarantee that you would win. This is a perfect example that regardless of the decision you made, there was still an element of chance that was involved which determined the final outcome.

If we make the analogy that we are in fact dealing with a series of random outcomes of dice rolls to determine our character, situations, values, and results, then it is a logical conclusion that the above blackjack situation CAN and WILL occur in our own lives. Our game strategy, then, is to make the best choices that we can to help increase the probability of good things happening to us. We can work hard to increase our skills to bump up those dice numbers as much as we can, but there will always be dice out there that we simply can't control and results we can never guarantee.

Let's take this concept of unfairness back to our randomness of our core attributes. Another funny thing about these dice of life is that we have no idea what we rolled. We may not even know they exist. But we generally start to figure some of them out pretty quickly.

Some kids in school start to wonder why Santa Claus only visits the rich kids. Some kids wonder why they're treated differently if their skin is a different color. Some children get picked last for the soccer team so they believe they are just not as athletic as the other kids. Even if it's not true, they now grow up believing that.

It's not fair that a mother can take good care of her health during pregnancy and still lose a child.

It's not fair that someone could be falsely accused of something and spend time in jail for a crime they didn't commit.

It's not fair if you're injured in an accident and the drunk driver walked away without a scrape.

Distribution Of Good and Bad Rolls

If we look at ourselves and our environments through the lens of the dice, it begins to make sense why these unfair things start to happen. It's easy to see that much of what occurs to us is determined by random circumstances that are simply outside of our control. It's only a matter of time before certain numbers will come up high or low on those chaotic dice. Ultimately, it's the result of the unchangeable law of probability. Now consider how many people there are in the world against that statistical distribution range. With so many people tossing dice against so many environments and situations, some of them are statistically bound to win, while others must come up short.

For every genius, there is an idiot on the other side of that middle line. For every lucky good break, there must be an equally poor one. For the elements in life we can't control, 1s are being rolled just as often as 6s and there is nothing we can do about it.

Unfortunately, given enough time and circumstances, the dice will inevitably give us terrible results. Tyrants like Hitler, Stalin, and Pol Pot will always be possible and bound to occur. But on the high and positive side, statistics also guarantees us that we will be blessed with certain gifts that will contribute unbelievable advancements to humanity: people like Michelangelo, Einstein, Isaac Newton, and Beethoven.

Every once in a while, someone is born in just the right time in the right place with just the right skills. They roll a big time Yahtzee and humanity itself gets a win. THAT is an encouraging thought.

Questions to consider:

- What events in your life can be identified as a bad luck dice roll?

- What events in your life can be identified as a good luck dice roll?

- What skill upgrades did you accomplish that helped your chances in getting a win?

7

Getting Motivated

Motivation is what causes us to do something. Once we determine our values and direction, it's the driving action we take to upgrade our skills to get there.

There is no shortage of motivational books and videos that are available for us to get pumped up about something. Some of them are helpful and can provide great insight. Maybe you've seen a celebrity or powerful speaker that shouts at us with some great advice and encouragement. Usually, these talks come with great clinical research and several real-world examples. They can be a fantastic resource to get you out of bed and ready to face the world. But how well do they really work? Why doesn't our life seem to change that much after getting yelled at by a movie star? Why do we feel like losers and failures when it doesn't work out? From the perspective of the dice, I think there are some key principles that can help explain this.

See, it's all about upgrading the skills. It doesn't always matter what we know or feel, but what we can do. It's not possible to learn how to ride a bicycle from reading a book. We can't watch a video about yoga and get the same benefits. We need to put in the time, effort, and energy to upgrade our abilities. There's no shortcut here. We need education. We need practice. We need experience. Oftentimes, watching a video or reading a book simply doesn't give you that. Those tools can certainly guide you in the right direction, but we need to set up the foundational habits and practice them until they become second nature. Only then can we have the foundation to build other skills that will get us closer to our goal.

Getting Started

When you write your name, you probably don't slow down and think about writing each letter. At one time you probably did, but you've done it so many times, now your hand may be able to just do it automatically without thinking. That's a skill that you've moved from a 1 to a 6 and it's a perfect example of what it means to upgrade our skills and abilities. What about tying your shoe or typing on a keyboard? We need to master these skills first, so we can master others.

Oftentimes we need to change the purpose of our motivation from the goal itself to the skills distinctly needed to get there. It's almost always necessary to set the foundation first. Roll over before you can crawl before you can walk before you can run. The proficiency in those core skills and abilities are truly what increases the probability of us succeeding in the final goal. That's why mastering the fundamentals is critical in any sport or hobby.

This is also why it's a huge advantage to know yourself. It's critical to have a good understanding of what your core skills and abilities are *before* you set off to reach a goal. Listening to the advice of a coach or an expert is absolutely necessary to learn, but it becomes even more valuable when you can cater the advice and guidance to yourself and your own unique situation. Leverage what you do well. Focus on improving a core skill where you may lack. Always play your own game with your own character.

However, what if a core skill we lack is motivation itself? What if you don't have any values? What if you don't have the desire or willpower to upgrade anything? Do you have any determination at all? What about grit, focus, or patience? Are those skills the result of more dice rolls and skill upgrades that we need to deal with? I would say most likely yes. It's reasonable to assume that people have varying degrees of focus and persistence. Not everyone can obtain the same level of energy and achievement capacity. This is more evidence that everyone is starting from a different position in the race and that comparing your progress or values to someone else isn't always a fair assessment. Again, the presence of so many dice doesn't create the same starting character or even the same game board.

The real secret to success is to develop the discipline that forces you to continue something during times when you're not motivated. That's why developing good habits is so important. Good habits put our daily routines on autopilot so there's no discussion or decision making about what needs to be done. Good habits force us to continue the healthy patterns even when we're not motivated to do so.

Choose Your Hard

Let's use the dice to explore a completely different angle of how to get motivated. Time for another one of dad's catch phrases:

> *Marriage is hard. Divorce is hard. Choose your hard.*
> *Obesity is hard. Being fit is hard. Choose your hard.*
> *Being in debt is hard. Being financially disciplined is hard. Choose your hard.*
> *Communication is hard. Not communicating is hard. Choose your hard.*
> *Life will never be easy. It will always be hard. But we can choose our hard. Pick wisely.   -Unknown*

This is a famous motivational quote that I often turn to. It forces us to make some key decisions about what battles we are willing to fight based on our core values. It's yet another reminder that there is no easy way out no matter what road we take. We can only hope that we are wise enough to choose the best options and disciplined enough to have the strength to fight for them.

However, I chose this quote for a reason because there is another side of this equation that often gets ignored. That particular statement directly falls into the theme of our random dice rolling.

What if you don't get to choose your hard?

What if you were born with or suddenly given a handicap? What if you get diagnosed with a terminal disease or cancer? What if you were abused as a child? Or experienced some horrible trauma that you are now forced to deal with every day? What if you were born with a mental illness where you spend each day in abject terrified horror?

Suddenly you find yourself looking at the dice in front of you and seeing very low numbers in MANY categories. You didn't choose that! Depending on your perspective, this simple quote can quickly turn from being motivational to downright insulting. Again, it's not fair.

Remember: your situation, goals, values, and resources can directly be the result of factors outside your control. That's the randomness of the dice that are thrown at us. By no means does that mean we give up! But I think it is encouraging to understand this reality when we evaluate our situation.

Always Think Ahead

A buddy of mine often tells this joke which I love: A man had an ultimate lifetime goal of living to be 100 years old. He went straight to the doctor for the best advice and asked: "Doctor! Will I live to be 100 years old??"

Doctor: "Do you smoke?"
Man: "Of course not!"
Doctor: "Well, do you drink any alcohol?"
Man: "No."
Doctor: "Do you eat any sugary treats or junk food?"
Man: "Not at all!"
Doctor: "Do you take drugs and party with wild women?"
Man: "No way!"
Doctor: "Then why would you want to?"

This is a funny reminder that I often use to justify the occasional health sin, especially in emergencies. But there is a strong lesson to be learned here that we can use for some long-term health related motivation.

The biggest drawback of our physical bodies is that we only get one. We're given only one chance to make this feeble bag of fatty meat work for as long as it can. Kids have no concept of this, and I long miss the days of feeling indestructible. But as we get older, our bodies begin to break down, pieces start to fall off, it hurts to stand up, and every day starts to feel like leg day. Even sneezing becomes terrifying.

Not only do I want to live a long time, but I also want my body to feel as good as possible in those later years while I'm doing it. It's hard to be sickly later in life. It's hard to take care of ourselves now to prevent it. Choose our hard? Our physical and mental health is indeed something some of us are fortunate enough to have a choice about. Feeling great in those later years of life is never guaranteed because of these forsaken dice. But personally, I want to increase the odds of that happening as much as possible.

I'm not afraid of dying. I'm afraid of being alive and not being able to live.

If You Don't Want To Do It For Yourself, Then Do It For Someone Else

If we want to improve our chances in any of this, we always need to find ways to get motivated. The goal here is to upgrade our dice and therefore our probabilities of getting a win. So, instead of the usual motivational talk about how you should suck it up and work hard, let's look at this concept from a completely different angle that I believe relates to our dice analogy.

The Dice of Life

Movie time: "*Good Will Hunting*". The premise is about a super genius kid (Matt Damon) growing up in the rough ghetto streets of south Boston trying to reconcile the apparent curse of his gift against his not-so-privileged life. There are about a dozen fantastic scenes in this movie that I could spend all day talking about, but one that illustrates this point is when his best friend Chuckie (Ben Affleck) finally confronts him about the reality of his situation. One day, Chuckie plainly lays it out for him: he has been given this wonderful gift, and neglecting to take advantage of it is essentially an insult to him and the people around them. Chuckie goes on to explain that the best part of his day is hoping that one day Will would just not be there. He is earnestly hoping that Will would simply take his rare gift, make something glorious out of it, and get out of that neighborhood, even if that means leaving his best friend behind.

My wife was raised in the shadow of her overachieving Ironman father. Like him, she grew up learning how to harness intense physical training to resolve any kind of stress and it quickly became her best form of therapy. However, after years of intense emotional stress, having tough children, and both mental and physical illnesses, her body finally broke down. All the physical activities she was so good at and loved to do were one day no longer an option to enjoy. She now lives in chronic pain where sometimes even the most basic tasks are unfairly difficult. She can no longer bike, swim, run, and often struggles to even walk. Ironically, her best outlet for dealing with her condition was taken away from her. Again, it's not fair.

She now lives in a situation where her skill and ability has essentially been downgraded from a 5 to about a 2. This was not by her choice, but the current battle is to now accept that new situation. That doesn't mean she gives up and doesn't do anything. It just means that she must adjust her goals and create different expectations for her distinct situation. There's nothing wrong with that. In fact, the effort should be celebrated! Downgrading happens all the time for a variety of dice reasons. For example: getting out of practice, changes in life circumstances, or even just naturally losing ability over time as we get older. It's frustrating when we need to work out twice as hard to get half the results, but that doesn't mean we give up.

Sometimes when I go jogging in the morning, I often make the mistake of complaining and moaning about how hard and horrible a chore it is. Maybe I whine a little bit about how cold and tired I am, but I quickly remind myself how lucky I am to even be able to get out there and do that. Not everyone can. I just need to look at my wife who often hides back the tears because she wishes she could get out and exercise just like before. Sure, I get many benefits from exercising, but she's the real reason I do it.

Absolutely do everything you can to make the hard choices to improve your life, and if for some reason you can't seem to get motivated to do something difficult for yourself, <u>then do it for the people who wish they had a choice.</u>

A Success Story?

Growing up I was one of those kids who seemed to struggle in school. I was never a very good test taker and usually procrastinated as much as I could. I was that kid who scrambled to finish his homework about 40 seconds before it was due, if I did it at all. It wasn't fun for me to read so I avoided doing any schoolwork as much as possible. The one thing I seemed to do decently well at was spatial reasoning and mechanical puzzles. For some reason at the time, I could solve a Rubik's cube in under 60 seconds, but I had enormous difficulty memorizing my spelling homework.

I remember in 4th grade there was a special honors program at my elementary school. Needless to say, I didn't even come close to qualifying. For a few hours each week, the selected "gifted" kids in the school would get out of class and march down to the library where they would meet for this special advanced program. Once there, they would work on extra projects which were beyond what we were learning in class. It was just something fun to challenge them because the normal schoolwork was apparently too easy. These extra projects usually consisted of a page of riddles or graphical math problems that were way beyond what they had already been taught in our regular class. They of course struggled with these things but the first thing they did after that class was to hand them to me. I could usually figure them out during lunch. I distinctly remember handing those papers back to them on their way back to the library while I went back to the 'normal' classroom.

Luckily, this ability I had didn't go unnoticed by most of my friends and family. I was fortunate to get quite a bit of encouragement and good advice about this. Growing up I heard plenty of: "You should be an engineer!" or "You're so gifted at spatial reasoning! You would be a great engineer!". With that encouragement, it was an easy decision for me to pursue an engineering degree going into college. There was little doubt about my path since I knew early on in my life that this was what I was meant to do. I started out ok, but academically, things went south fairly quickly. About halfway through my sophomore year, I was in significant danger of flunking out. My situation started to get very serious, and I made the ultimate decision to finally apply myself. That was it. No more slacking off! In one of my courses, we had a mid-term exam coming up that would essentially make or break my academic career. I turned on the gas.

For three solid weeks, I studied harder than I had ever studied before. I never left my room. I worked through every example in the book multiple times. I practiced every example problem I could find with extreme confidence. I was never more focused and prepared for anything in my life ever. The test day finally came.

I absolutely killed it! I chuckled to myself because it was the easiest test ever! Because of how much I studied and prepared, every question was so simple I breezed right through them. I was the first one done with the test and I even had plenty of time to go back to triple check everything just to be sure all my answers made sense. It was at that moment I finally understood. I finally knew what it was like to focus, put in the hard work, and get rewarded. All those people that supported me along the way were right. Somehow, they all knew I could do it if I just decided to apply myself.

We found out the next day that the test was in fact too easy. There were about 35 kids in the class and 12 of them got a 100%. There would obviously be no curve and the teacher actually apologized for not making the exam difficult enough. I knew it was too good to be true and that hard work was overkill after all. No matter. I was back on track, psyched up, and fully proud of my newfound confidence.

He handed my test back to me. I looked down and saw a big fat 26%. Yes, 26%. I remember that moment very clearly because that 26% was written in extra large numbers at the top of the first page and had a giant red circle around it. My entire life just stopped. I physically couldn't process what had just happened. All my life I was told that I was meant to do this. I did everything I could think of to prepare. That's not what that motivational video said would happen. That's not what was supposed to happen if I worked hard and didn't give up. I didn't understand what went wrong and had absolutely no idea what to do.

Yes, this is the worst motivational story ever. Nobody ever tells stories like this because it's sad and it's NOT what we want to hear. I remember hearing one time about life not being fair. I remember something about getting bad luck dice rolls. Stories like this one are not printed in those self-help and motivational books. But these are the stories that often happen to us in real life, and when these things happen, they can be very isolating and make us feel like complete failures. So, if this kind of thing happens to you, it's important to know that you are NOT alone. In fact, situations like this are probably way more common than the glorious success stories we usually hear about on the talk shows.

However, you still may be curious to know what happened to me after that moment. The very next day I marched into the admissions office and changed my major to something called Architectural Studies. I knew I still wanted to design and build something so I thought Architecture would be the next best thing. It turns out I was not very artistic and if I did want to be an Architect, that would be another 5 years of college in a special dedicated school. By then it was then my 5th year of college and I was basically starting over. I tallied up my credits and changed my plan yet again to something called Information Science. I chose that major simply because it was the quickest way I could graduate and get the heck out of there. At the time, I had a part time job at the campus computer lab, so I at least had some training on how to do some basic PC troubleshooting. I figured every company needed some sort of IT work or computer repair so I was hoping that decision would make it easier to find a job.

Then came the dreaded programming class. Of course, it was a requirement, so I couldn't get out of it. In case you didn't already know this, pretty much every normal person hates computer programming. It's awful and I was horrible at it. It didn't make sense and it was totally not what I wanted to do. I struggled yet again and spent most of my evenings getting more and more frustrated at the world. But then one night I was working on a homework project which was to build some sort of a basic calculator program. In some weird awkward random moment, something clicked. It was the strangest sensation that I'll never forget. Suddenly, I stopped looking at the code on the screen and I started to visualize in my mind what the code was doing. My mind was now instantly able to convert the letters and characters on the screen into actual shapes and objects that I *could* understand. No longer was I looking at computer code. All I saw in front of me was a huge bag of Legos that I could use to build anything I wanted. I could now visualize an entire design in my mind, collect the pieces I needed, and just type it out. I saw how modules and functions worked together. If I needed a tool that didn't exist, I could build one. I very quickly learned how databases work and could see tables and data objects as nothing more than simple building blocks. By the end of the semester, everyone wanted to see what I could come up with and I was basically teaching the class.

After that moment, it became very clear that's where my career would be headed. No longer would I be a physical engineer like everyone thought I would. But I would use those same core skills to become a software architect using computer code and data science instead of metal, glass, and concrete.

What does this story have to do about the dice? As it turns out, pretty much everything. I first got lucky with one of my dice having a great natural skill and ability. I then got a good dice roll with people around me who recognized it and encouraged me to use it. A bad dice roll came up with what I thought I was supposed to do. But I had good foundational computer skills and work habits that allowed me to acquire more advanced skills that I wasn't even planning for. I worked hard to upgrade many of my skills along the way that increased my probabilities of finding something that eventually worked for me, but how much of my eventual success was my effort? And how much of it was due to getting lucky in that computer class one day?

I often wonder what would have happened if I had stuck with Engineering. Would I have eventually made it? Should I have read that motivational book again and stuck to it? We're told that we're not supposed to give up on our dreams so maybe I should have stayed the course like they said? Should I have learned my lesson sooner and changed majors earlier? There's really no way to know because we're throwing these dice everywhere, and sometimes they turn out to give you something you least expect.

Different Methods and Sources Of Motivation

Overall, it becomes important to understand that motivation itself looks inherently different for everyone. Just like any other dice that are influencing us, people can be motivated in different ways for a variety of reasons. Depending upon our unique values, brain chemistry, and abilities, it's also fair to say that people would have different intensities of motivation as well. It's a curious phenomenon to see how some humans can be so intense about achieving a particular goal, while others don't even seem to care or bother with it. Even motivation itself looks like another example of more dice to deal with. I often wonder if motivation itself is one of those core foundational skills that we can upgrade.

Questions to consider:

- What gets you motivated to work hard toward your goals?

- What random dice rolls have impacted the results when trying to accomplish your goals? Were some good? Were some bad?

- Which hard do you choose?

8

Survivorship Bias

Survivorship Bias is the tendency for us to only look at the successful outcomes of a given distribution or process. I think this concept plays a role in looking at how we can better understand our chances of succeeding at the challenges we decide to take on in this game.

During my short tour of duty in business boot camp, I was always on the lookout for the hidden secret of success. What was the one trick that would do it? What do you NEED to do to make it big? What was the one thing that all the great business leaders had in common that was the key to make their success possible?

Fail Fast, Fail Often

During one of the many motivational seminars, I finally heard the answer. The speaker was a highly successful CEO of an enormous company and of course had an unbelievably impressive resume. You may have heard of it, but his sage advice was: "Fail Fast, Fail Often."

The essence of this popular technique is that you are inevitably going to fail. Of course, you shouldn't try to, but it's going to happen, so we need to learn how to best deal with it. The trick here is to learn as much as you can and apply those lessons as quickly as possible. Expect defeat as just a necessary part of the process. Fail fast, learn fast, so you can try again as soon as you are able. Change something, adjust, and try again. Simply don't waste precious time and resources on something that doesn't work. The similar phrase we often hear is: "The definition of insanity is to do the same thing over and over again expecting a different result."

This concept totally makes sense from our dice rolling perspective. The more chances we take, the better our chances of rolling something that works. Faster rolls mean even more chances and an increase in the probability of hitting something big. Getting stuck on something that doesn't work is the kryptonite of any business or task. It makes perfect sense.

Don't Give Up

Then came the story of Harland Sanders. This guy did things very differently. He was 65 years old and completely broke, but he liked to cook, so he decided to try to sell one of his recipes to some family and friends in an attempt to pay his rent. It didn't work. He tried again, and it still didn't work. The rumored estimate was that he made over 1,000 attempts to sell his chicken recipe to anyone he could find. Then, on the 1,010th time someone finally said yes (probably just to shut him up) and the franchise began. Yes, Colonel Sanders Kentucky Fried Chicken was the result of some old desperate broke man going door to door trying to sell something that nobody liked or wanted.

The moral of this success story is about never giving up! It's never too late! Even when times are tough and the odds are stacked against you, NEVER EVER quit!

So, Which Is It?

Now wait a minute! If you're paying attention, these two business strategies somewhat contradict each other. Here I was trying to learn the secret and I was getting conflicting answers. Should I "fail fast"? Or "never give up"? This contradiction really bothered me for a long time.

I think the answer lies once again in our dice of probability. For some reason, we only seem to hear about the winners. We always hear about the guy that accomplished something great and we become fascinated with how they did it. We celebrate that success and try to get all the advice and secrets we can. But we rarely hear about the guy that pretty much did the exact same thing and it DIDN'T work.

Is Luck Possible?

It's quite possible (and probable) that some luck was involved in the outcomes that led to the victory. Something random may have happened along the way that could have been a real contribution for success. We must remember that we're rolling a lot of dice here. Maybe the right person was in the right place at the right time? Maybe their opponent made a mistake at a crucial time? Maybe a critical person on the other end of the phone happened to be in a good mood that day of the sale? I think sometimes we are reluctant to admit that it wasn't always ALL our doing.

I'm sure you've heard many stories that involve some sort of miraculous event that happened at the last minute that caused everything to work out. We love those stories because they prove that all the hard work and perseverance paid off in the end. At the last minute, they got the call to get the job. On their last try they finally made the sale that they desperately needed. For some reason, you'll rarely hear the stories about the failures. I guess we don't like those stories, so we tend to ignore them, but that doesn't mean they're not there.

Humans tend to be very egotistical and it's not very often they concede that they got lucky with something that may have happened to them. We are always proud of our hard work and usually want to take the credit for all the great things that have happened. Pride is an easy place to go and it often blinds us. Most likely a few people helped along the way that we acknowledge in our speech, but we inherently want to believe that we have complete control over our situations, and that it was MOSTLY our hard work that was responsible for getting us where we are. We

WANT life to work that way because it helps give us that comforting sense of ownership and control.

Can you imagine at the end of a motivational video if the speaker said: "Do this, this, and this. Work hard, don't give up, and all your dreams will come true! Oh and by the way, sometimes you have to get lucky." That probably wouldn't fly as a popular piece of advice, but would it be wrong?

Remember, it's very possible to increase our probabilities of winning through upgrading our education and experience. It's a huge advantage and necessary that we do that. Hard work and perseverance for any goal are almost *always* required. Our goal must be to become fully prepared and have the skills to take advantage of any luck when we get it. The more experience and skills we learn, the more likely we are to identify opportunities of luck and take advantage of them. But the underlying presence of some luck on our journey should never be discounted.

"Winning the lottery is easy! You can do it too! Just buy a ticket!"
Says the guy who won the lottery…

We Only Study The Winners

There is a classic example of survivorship bias that is worth exploring here. Dean Yeong has a brilliant summary about this in one of his popular articles that really can't be summarized any better.

The Dice of Life

Directly from his article: "Survivorship Bias: What World War II Taught Us About Our Mental Flaws":

"During World War II, researchers from the Center for Naval Analyses conducted a study on the damage done to returned aircraft after missions. They then recommended adding armor to the areas that showed the most damage to minimize bomber losses to enemy fire.

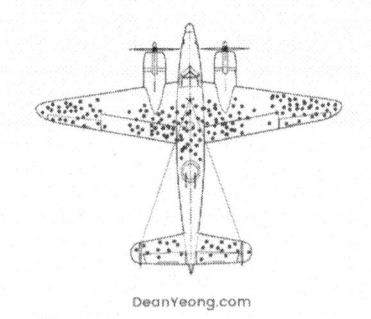

However, Abraham Wald suggested differently.

Wald was a Hungarian mathematician and a member of the Statistical Research Group (SRG), where he applied his statistical skills to various wartime problems.

He noted that the study was only conducted on the aircraft that had survived their missions. It didn't paint a complete picture when the bombers that had been shot down were not presented for the damage assessment.

With that, the holes in the returning aircraft were areas that need no extra armor — since the bombers could take damage and still return safely. On the other hand, the areas where the returning aircraft were unscathed are those areas that, if hit, would cause the plane to crash and be lost.

Wald then proposed that the Navy reinforce the undamaged areas by adding more armor to them — which was a perfect demonstration of how to not fall prey to the survivorship bias."

Only looking at "successful" people doesn't give us a clear understanding of the whole picture. What about the people that failed or didn't win? Did they do something wrong? Did they not work hard enough? Were there other factors that may have contributed to the situation that we ignored or just couldn't see?

I'm convinced that the random probabilities of our dice play a role here. (Or they have a "roll" to play since I'm compelled to insert the gratuitous dad joke.)

So this phenomenon tends to align with what we noticed in the beginning. This goes back to our tendency to only look at the people who rolled all 6's. We tend to compare ourselves to the top few percent of the random distribution. It's certainly a great source of inspiration to be looking in that direction, but that's simply not the statistical reality of the situation.

The Dice of Life

There are essentially two hidden metrics of success involved here:

1. The luck of skills and what skill levels you initially received. Not everyone begins the journey with the same skills or potential.

2. The situational luck that contributed to a success: events that happened (or didn't happen) which may have occurred during our struggles that we can't always control.

Understanding that perspective shines a much different light on setting our expectations vs. the reality of guaranteed success.

Questions to consider:

- Do you ever catch yourself only looking at the "winners"?

- Can you think of any examples of people that won something while using what's considered a poor strategy?

- Can you think of any examples where you've gotten conflicting advice about something?

9

The Dark Dice

Perhaps the most dangerous and the most difficult adversaries that humans must deal with in our living adventure game are the elusive challenges of Cognitive Disabilities and Mental Illnesses. These problems include, but are not limited to: depression, anxiety, social or learning disorders, psychotic disorders, addictions, personality disorders, or trauma induced disorders. There's a very good chance that someone in your life that may be dealing with one of these issues in some way. If you don't know anyone, then someone you know is working REALLY hard to hide it. If you are the one that happens to be struggling with one of these issues, you unfortunately know exactly what I'm talking about.

We often didn't choose them. And many people go through their lives not even knowing they are there. These are the dice that we may have no idea that we rolled or that if they even exist. Most of us barely understand them and they can be difficult if not impossible to discuss or even think about. What we do know is that they are directly responsible for making lives exponentially more difficult for many of the victims of these problems. Many of these disabilities and illnesses are simply bad rolls with bad numbers. The term Dark Dice is most fitting.

For the people who may have unfortunately rolled high numbers on these mysterious dice, they are a force that can easily trump everything else in their life. They are an instant toxic downgrade that affects their ability to function and upgrade almost every other skill. It's no exaggeration that people with these challenges can spend their entire lives attempting to improve their skills only to reach the same point of the race where someone else started. Because of this, the rest of us really need to cut them some slack.

But probably the worst aspect of mental health issues is that the people that need the most help are often the least enabled to get it. All too often, they lack the ability to fight for themselves.

Ignoring Is Always Easiest

Unfortunately, the easiest and most common way for many people to deal with these types of issues is to ignore them. They are simply NOT convenient. Again, it doesn't help that many of them are so difficult to identify and understand. The most common reaction is to usually turn away from that person and hope someone else can deal with the problem. Remember, people want to think of the human body as just a predictable machine. Of course, that approach is so much easier! But the elusive elements of mental and cognitive health issues immediately throw a wrench into that naive belief.

The human brain is anything but a mechanical robot made of gears and levers. We've made incredible strides learning what the different parts of the brain do and how they control some basic functions. However, as a whole, it remains a chaotic soup of chemicals, hormones, and electrical impulses that we are only beginning to understand. As humans, we live in a flowing river of emotions, thoughts, and feelings that could never possibly be the same between two people. It's only a matter of time and chance that something may go wrong with that delicate chemical balance, and that we suffer the consequences of a possibly serious disorder.

Awareness and Education

Awareness and education are some of the best starting points of action in making these types of issues better understood. I can only hope that using the analogy of some of the dice concepts from this book may give someone a better perspective and understanding of the subject.

1. Be aware that these "Dark Dice" exist. It is critical that we avoid going about our lives pretending that they just aren't there. Just like people are born with natural characteristics like genetic health, who your parents were, or a talent for music, these dice can get rolled just as easily and get mixed in with everything else. Ignoring them is an unacceptable option.

2. Be very careful when you say you 'understand'. Everyone experiences panic or depression at some point. But that doesn't mean you are suffering from a disorder. People often make the mistake of thinking that

experiences like that are what victims of these disorders are going through. A severe disabling diagnosis is a VERY different thing than a fleeting feeling or a temporary passing sad mood. These disorders are no joke and will shut down a life. They can be relentless waves of pain and hopelessness that will completely disable your ability to function. It's important to <u>not fall into a number bias</u> when dealing with someone that has a mental illness.

3. Education: Whether you are struggling with a mental illness, depression, or know someone that is, education can be the first and best ally in coping with this type of challenge. It's critically important that you get the best information from the right people. The more you know about it, the less scary it becomes, and the better decisions can be made about recovery and treatment options.

4. Continue to avoid "Number Bias". Remember that we tend to think people should act and think the same way we do. The same great advice may not be suitable for people who rolled some of these dark dice. Our worldview and our experience are coming from a perspective that doesn't apply to someone's brain that may be working so much differently. What is great advice for one person, may be dangerous for someone else with these conditions. Take the time to find out and learn what they need, not what you THINK they need. For someone with serious depression, that "glass half full" lecture is insulting and not helpful.

5. Get help. And make sure it is the *right* help. Getting the wrong therapy in these situations may not be productive or can even make the situation worse. That's

why education is so important in understanding the various kinds of illnesses and the different types of therapies available.

6.   Be patient. It cannot be understated how long and difficult the journey is to live with an illness like these. Recovery can take a massive amount of time and forgiveness. Treatments can take months, years, or even decades. Remember it is not always their fault and most often the bad luck of the dice is the thing to blame.

7.   Empower them with support, resources, and love. For people dealing with these issues, it can feel like the equivalent of running a marathon every day. It is physically and mentally exhausting and can be unbelievably lonely. It can't be understated how important it is to be supported and loved through the tough times.

The good news is that like any other skill, many of these situations can usually be improved. With some practice and training, it's often very possible to upgrade a struggling mental health situation. Learning the right tools and techniques can be powerful habits in training your brain chemistry into functioning better. For the most part, our brains act similarly to a muscle that could use some extra exercising. Just because you rolled a 2, doesn't mean you have to stay there.

Knowing these concepts may make it easier for us to have compassion for, to understand, and to forgive others who could be struggling with these issues. Again, people are living with different dice rolls which may not entirely be their fault. They're playing on a very different gameboard.

The Dice of Life

I like to think that understanding the dice analogy can be a great way to help people understand the reasons why humans operate and behave so differently. I think it's important to know that we are all at the mercy of so many random forces. The domain of mental health issues is a very clear illustration of how humans are often the victims of so many different dice rolls, both good and bad.

Questions to consider:

- Who do you know that struggles or may be struggling with a clinical mental health disorder?

- Do you ever talk with them about it to attempt to understand what they need and what they're going through?

- When you see someone struggling, do you ignore the situation and write them off as 'crazy'? Or do you imagine them having a handicap they are suffering with?

10

Putting It All Together

The dice serve as a great analogy to help explain the different aspects of human diversity and the varied degrees of personal perspectives and prosperity. We are all born with a unique set of circumstances, talents, aptitudes, and characteristics, each with different levels of abilities and potential. Many of these we may be able to improve and upgrade along the way. but for some of these, we will always be at the mercy of what we have originally been given.

As we grow through life, we are continually being shaped and molded by yet another set of random circumstances. These dice include our environment, social influences, education, people, and events that occur to us during our life. They have an enormous impact on creating our values, morals, and motivations. Some of these elements we can control, others we cannot, but there is no escaping the endless stream of dice coming at us that we must navigate. Our worldview is created from the accumulation of both random circumstances and the skills we acquire along the way.

No matter our efforts, many successes of our journey will always be at the mercy of an unknown outcome. Our goal can never be to guarantee the results, but only to maximize (or minimize) the probability of what occurs.

How the Dice Work

A single standard 6-sided die gives us a random number between 1 and 6. That random number gives us a particular value within the possible range. Rolling a 1 will always have the same probability of rolling a 6. We use the dice as an analogy to represent all the components and situations of our initial being, developmental challenges, and skill level progressions.

Build Your Character

Our starting character in this game of life is initially given to us by a process of random distribution. Much like the chaotic results of the dice, many of our natural skills, situations, and aptitudes are determined by factors beyond our control. All these variables make us who we are and what capabilities and liabilities we initially have to work with.

In regard to applying those random probabilities in our life adventure, the dice rolling analogy comes from three basic domains:

The Dice of Life

1. Natural Born Characteristics: These are the random elements that we are born with and have no control over. Examples include our parents, where we were born, and any naturally born aptitudes, abilities, and liabilities. Because of the physical mathematical rules of probabilities, some humans will receive the highest value combinations of natural circumstances. Others will begin the journey with a much less favorable starting point and potential.

2. Skills and Abilities: These are the skills that we learn and enhance during our life. A numeric value on the dice can be used to represent our skill level for each of them. Depending on our values, we try to upgrade them to increase our proficiency. "Level up" in a sense. Leveling up gives us a higher number and increases our probability of getting a win with whatever challenge we face. They can come in two basic forms:

    A. Hard Skills: A learned external skill that is used to accomplish a goal or task. This can be a job, hobby, or some activity where skill level can be measured with a range of progression.

    B. Soft Skills: Internal skills that are just as important, but can be a bit harder to define a range of expertise. Examples might include Patience, Kindness, Determination, Empathy, or Wisdom.

3. Events and Circumstances: These are the random situations that occur to us throughout our life journey. They can be good, neutral, or bad. We maximize the expertise in our skill levels to handle them when they come.

The Game Board

Our brief time here on this planet is equivalent to the concept of an adventure-type game board, which is also determined by yet another set of random probabilities. We like to think that we have control over our own objectives and goals, and that we are the ones who decide how we are going to play and what challenges we take on. Sometimes those goals and values are given to us by other people. Sometimes we may determine our own path. The reality is that because of our unique character, worldview, and circumstances, the underlying game board and objectives are inherently different for everyone.

What obstacles might we have that other people don't?

What skills does our character have that may give us an advantage or disadvantage? Will they influence our decision making about what path we choose to take?

Upgrades

The good news is that we're not stuck with many of our dice roll values. If we put in the time and work, we can increase our skill levels in many areas. By learning and practicing, we essentially upgrade our point values making us stronger in those skills. Many goals in life require a high proficiency spanning several skill sets. The more we can upgrade, the better chance we have at succeeding and winning!

Because of our natural abilities and other learned skills, people will also progress and upgrade their skill proficiency at different rates. Some people simply have higher 'ceilings' than others. And because people have different arrays of core values and motivations, they will focus on upgrading dissimilar skill sets to perhaps achieve very different goals.

Number Bias

We can only perceive the world from our own point of view. Our individual perception is based on the unique combination of our past experiences, skill sets, and circumstances. Along our journey we learn certain truths about how the world works and how we should interact with it. We call this perspective a number bias because we tend to think everyone else is operating with the same dice rolls that we have. We also then naturally expect that everyone should essentially have the same values and goals that we do.

Humans also tend to project their own reality onto other people. We naively assume they are playing with the same character on the same game board. We tend to think other humans experience the same problems we do and in the same way. Our firsthand experience also causes us to think that other people should have the same results that we did.

We also tend to gravitate towards people that share our values and abilities. People like to associate with others who share a common unspoken language that helps confirm and justify our opinions and perspectives.

Life Isn't Fair

Because much of our lives are determined by random probability, it is inevitable that bad things will happen to us just as often as good ones. The laws of probability tell us that 1s will show up just as often as 6s. We can upgrade our skills as much as possible, but the final results will often be determined by the result of yet another random dice roll. You can upgrade all you want to a 5, but it's possible your opponent can still roll a 6. It's very possible to do everything right, and still lose.

Getting Motivated

If we want to give ourselves the best probability for success, it's important that we upgrade our skills as much as possible. But what actually drives us to do that? What causes us to make the decision to work hard and achieve those upgrades? If everything is indeed left up to chance, why bother?

The reasons for our motivation can vary as much as our personalities and values. Just like our skills and situations, people are motivated in different ways for different reasons. Just because you rolled a 2 in something, doesn't mean you have to stay there. It's always in our best interest to upgrade as much as possible to increase our chances for success.

Survivorship Bias

It's important for us to focus on the winners and learn what they did to succeed, but don't fall into the trap of ONLY focusing on the winners. Understand that often there are more factors involved. Because of the randomness of dice, it's actually impossible for everyone to succeed given the same challenges.

The journey always appears to be very clear for the people that win. But the real world often reminds us that not everyone will produce the same results for the same efforts. Again, all we can do is grow our skills to increase the probabilities that something may or may not occur.

The Dark Dice

Be aware of the dark dice of mental and emotional health. These dice are of course the most difficult to see and understand. Most of us probably carry a few of them that we may not even realize. For those who suffer severely with these issues, they can become an all-consuming challenge that distracts from everything else. Excelling in a career or in relationships becomes secondary when just getting through the day becomes the highest priority.

Fortunately, many of these dice can be upgraded like anything else. With the right tools, work, support, and practice, there is much hope to improve the quality of life for those that suffer with these issues.

Education and awareness are critical. Understanding these disorders allows us to fear them less, and to hopefully be more tolerant and forgiving of people that may suffer from them.

Common Applications

If you are a parent: Be aware of the natural abilities and limitations your children inherently carry with them. Be mindful when you 'compare' them to other siblings or children from a different family. Or even to your own childhood. Motivate them to explore their potential in a variety of skills, but also encourage them to have the fortitude to persevere whenever challenged. Upgrade their dice rolls as much as possible!

If you are an executive or manager in a business: Remind yourself that human employees are often not 'plug and play' objects. Skillsets, experience, and personality strengths are not always interchangeable for many tasks that need to be accomplished. As a leader, it's important to identify and leverage any natural abilities to maximize the potential of your team. Set the example as a leader and make it a goal to help employees become who they were meant to be in both a professional and personal capacity.

Personal interactions: ALWAYS make attempts to view the world through other perspectives. Instead of only focusing on right or wrong, take a moment and try to understand WHY someone believes or acts the way they do. Being aware of dice rolls can often help you view the situation from a much wiser position. Be mindful that many opinions are often based on factors outside someone's control. Yes, that includes our own perspectives as well.

Personal development: Get to know your dice! Develop a life-game strategy based on the specific strengths and weaknesses of your randomly generated character. Prioritize your upgrades, leverage your advantages, and devise a game plan that's aggressive but achievable for you.

Understand that you have a unique game board in front of you. Avoid trying to play someone else's game.

In Conclusion

The entire purpose of the dice analogy is to hopefully provide an illustration to some of the core reasons why humans are so fundamentally different. It's important to explore the principles of why we interact and behave so uniquely with each other and why we tackle the world in such different ways. Much of who we are and what we do comes from the randomness of the natural world around us and our own personal interactions with it. Hopefully the analogy of the dice provides us a new language and framework for discussing some of the reasons why humans act and behave the way they do. It's an interesting idea.

The dice help explain that we live within a range of possibilities of our skills, actions, and circumstances as well as the element of chaotic chance for both failure and success.

What did you roll?

ABOUT THE AUTHOR

Howard Minor is a happily married husband and proud father of three. He is a software engineer and database architect who has spent most of his professional career in healthcare I.T. consulting. Howard is a huge fan of Bitcoin and well known for his diverse skill set in a variety of random (and mostly useless) activities. He is a nationally ranked dart player, avid golfer, campfire guitar player, ballroom dancer, windsurfer, marathon runner, and can still solve a Rubik's cube in less than 25 seconds. Howard has recently branched out of his comfort zone and made an attempt to be an author.